Shelia Robinson
671-6121 call for
information
about course

American Red Cross
Lifeguard Training
Instructor's Manual

ISBN 0-86536-147-9

Acknowledgments

The Lifesaving Revision Advisory Committee of the American Red Cross provided the primary advice and guidance for the design and content of this revised *Lifeguard Training Instructor's Manual* and course.

The members of the committee included Reverend Rodney P. Bourg, St. Bernard Parish Red Cross Chapter, Chalmette, Louisiana; Paul M. Cerio, Supervisor of Aquatics, University of Nebraska, Omaha, Nebraska; Darwin DeLappa, Director, Water Safety, New York State Parks, Recreation and Historic Preservation, Albany, New York; Michael C. Giles, Aquatics Director, University of Southern Mississippi, Hattiesburg, Mississippi; Ralph Johnson, Director of Aquatics, Indiana Univeristy of Pennsylvania, Indiana, Pennsylvania; John Malatak, Officer, Health and Safety, American Red Cross, National Headquarters, Washington, D.C.; Jane W. McCharen, Metro Public Schools, Nashville, Tennessee; Mike Miller, Director of Aquatics, University of Missouri, Kansas City, Missouri; Michael T. Shellito, Department of Parks and Recreation, City of Roseville, Roseville, California; Marilyn Strom, Aquatics Director, University of Massachusetts–Boston, Boston, Massachusetts; Royce Van Evera, Director of Community Services, American Red Cross, Albany Area Chapter, Albany, New York; Lelia Vaughan, Recreation and Park Consultant, Jonesville, Texas.

Members of the development team at the American Red Cross national headquarters included Frank Carroll; Thomas C. Werts; and Martha Beshers. This *Instructor's Manual* was reviewed by Lawrence Newell, Ed.D. and Jon Martindale.

Contents

1 *Introduction*

This *American Red Cross Lifeguard Training Instructor's Manual* (Stock No. 329447) replaces the *Lifeguard Training Instructor's Manual* (Stock No. 321246) published in August 1983. This new manual reflects new and updated material presented in the *American Red Cross Lifeguard Training Supplement* (Stock No. 329448) developed to supplement the *American Red Cross Lifeguard Training* textbook, 1983, 1984 edition.

This manual is intended to serve as a resource for people who are certified by the American Red Cross to teach American Red Cross Lifeguard Training. Information and teaching suggestions are provided to help you plan and conduct the course effectively, according to Red Cross standards. You are expected to cover course topics as outlined and presented in this manual. You must be familiar with the material presented in the textbook, in the *Supplement,* and in the *Instructor's Manual* before you teach this course. In addition to teaching the Lifeguard Training course, you are qualified to teach the Lifeguard Training Review course. Requirements and guidelines for conducting the Lifeguard Training Review course are in Appendix F of this *Instructor's Manual.*

Course Objectives

- To ensure that participants become aware of and recognize the common hazards associated with various types of aquatic facilities and develop the knowledge and skills to eliminate or minimize such hazards
- To ensure that participants learn to recognize when a person is in a distress or drowning situation and to rescue that person
- To ensure that participants understand the lifeguard-employer, and lifeguard-patron relationships
- To provide explanations, demonstrations, practice, and review of the rescue skills essential for lifeguards
- To establish an awareness of the responsibilities of a lifeguard and instill an enthusiasm for carrying them out
- To develop participants' speed, endurance, and technique in swimming and lifeguarding skills

Course Characteristics

Participants must understand that the material presented in this course is general in nature and should be adapted to meet the needs of various aquatic facilities. This course is not intended to be a complete lifeguard training program.

Course Prerequisites

To enroll in the Lifeguard Training course, a person must—
- Be at least 15 years old.
- Swim 500 yards continuously using each of the following strokes for at least 50 yards each: crawl, breaststroke, elementary backstroke, sidestroke.
- Surface dive to a minimum depth of 9 feet and bring a 10-pound diving brick to the surface.
- Surface dive to a minimum depth of 5 feet and swim underwater for a minimum of 15 yards.
- Tread water for 1 minute.

These tests must be successfully completed before the end of Session 1.

Course Design

The content of the Lifeguard Training course is designed to be taught in eight sessions. These sessions are followed by two sessions, 9 and 10, that include the written examination and the skills tests. Session 1 content includes a course introduction and skills screening. Sessions 2 through 8 begin with a 5-minute review of the content of the previous session followed by discussion of the material in the reading assignments. Discussion usually lasts from 40 minutes to 1 hour. A 10-minute break follows the discussion, during which participants change clothes to prepare for skills practice. This practice usually takes about 2 hours. At the end of most skills practice, participants take a conditioning swim designed to improve their speed and endurance or to provide for the practice of the skills taught in previous sessions. A review of the session and a new reading assignment take up the final 5 minutes of every session except Sessions 9 and 10.

Assignments

Participants are expected to complete all reading assignments before the beginning of the next class period. The instructor may briefly review the content with participants or discuss it at some length, depending on the nature of the material and the time available, but it is the responsibility of the participants to have read the material beforehand and to be thoroughly familiar with it. Reading assignments are given at the end of the lesson plans for Sessions 1 through 7 in this manual. The instructor, however, may choose to give out these assignments just before the 10-minute break. An initial assignment—textbook: Preface and Chapters 1, 2, and 3, and *Supplement:* Chapter 1, pages 2 through 9—should be given to each participant to complete **before** they take Session 1.

Time and Certification Requirements

The time necessary to teach each session of this course varies from approximately 2 hours, 40 minutes to 3 hours. Total time for the course, including the final skills test and the written examination, but not including suggested audiovisuals, is approximately 27 hours. Using the audiovisuals, however, will enable the instructor to cut down on time otherwise allotted for discussion and demonstration. As a contingency for bad weather, additional sessions should be scheduled when the course is conducted at an outdoor facility.

Additional time may need to be scheduled to teach skills that are specific to waterfront facilities, such as practice in using rescue boats. Additional time may also need to be scheduled for practice in rescuing a scuba diver.

Times given in the outline and in the lesson plan for each session are based on the time required to teach 10 participants. With classes that have more than 10 participants, minimum course hours will need to be increased for each additional participant to allow for skills screening, practice, and final skills evaluation.

To ensure that participants are qualified to receive a certificate, the instructor must be confident that the participants have satisfactorily completed all of the requirements. Participants who are poorly trained may have a false opinion of their ability to carry out the duties of a lifeguard properly. Additional practice sessions may be required for participants with weak skills.

Either before taking the course or before graduating from it, participants are required to have—
* A current (within three years) American Red Cross Standard First Aid certificate (or equivalent) and

- A current (within one year) American Red Cross Adult CPR certificate (or equivalent).

Certification recognizes the successful completion of the Lifeguard Training course. To complete the course successfully, a participant must pass a final skills test and a written examination based on material presented in accordance with policies and procedures established by the American Red Cross. Certification is not intended to imply a form of licensure or to guarantee the future performance of the individual. It merely indicates that the participant has met the requirements established for the course.

Facilities

A swimming pool or other swimming area with a deep water area of 9 feet or more is recommended for conducting the prerequisite swimming skills tests, as well as for teaching the full course.

It is desirable to have a classroom in the immediate area. It should be equipped with all of the teaching aids and materials used to support the instruction. If a waterfront facility is used, it should be an open water, nonsurf area with sufficient space for skills practice.

Number of Participants

It is recommended that you have one instructor for every 10 participants in your class. If the class has more than 10 participants, you should have a co-instructor. Close supervision is required to ensure effective practice and the safety of participants. Furthermore, you can run a class more efficiently if you keep the class size reasonably small, and you are less likely to exceed the allotted time periods for various activities.

Patterns of Class Organization

Patterns of class organization are formations used to provide participants with the opportunity to develop a desired skill. Instructors should become thoroughly familiar with the common patterns of class organization, which include formations for discussions, demonstrations, drills in which the participants remain in one spot (static drills), and drills in which the participants move from one point to another (fluid drills). For descriptions of patterns of class organization, see Appendix E.

Lifeguard instructors must constantly strive to provide the maximum number of opportunities for skills practice for all participants during each class period. This involvement is essential if participants are to learn the required skills. Failure to keep participants actively involved can also cause participants to become chilled and restless, which can lead to a loss of class control.

Skills Practice Sessions

The skills practice sections of each session are designed to give participants the opportunity to observe demonstrations of each skill and then to practice until they can perform the skill correctly. A *Lifeguarding Skills Checklist* (Form 6608) for the instructor to use to check off skills as the participants perform them correctly is available from the local chapter. Appendix D is a sample of this form.

If there are additional co-instructors or instructor aides available, skills-practice sessions may be conducted using the station method. For example, stations can be set up for the practice of certain water rescue skills: at one station, participants practice working with a rescue tube and/or rescue buoy; at a second station, participants practice using a rescue board; and at a third station, participants practice removing a victim from the water.

Participants receive instruction and are allowed time to practice skills at each station. At the end of a predetermined time, participants move to the next station. The number of co-instructors and instructor aides required is determined by the number of stations. In the most desirable situation, only instructors are station leaders.

Small Group Sessions and Special Assignments

Lifeguards must be able to relate to their fellow staff members and to the facility patrons. They must be able to communicate in a knowledgeable and courteous manner. A lifeguard must also be able to accept direction and constructive criticism. To assist participants with the development of communication skills, instructors may conduct portions of the course, if time and class size permit, with the class divided into small groups (three to four participants) for problem-solving exercises and presentations. These may also be conducted as special assignments to be completed outside the class period.

The basic purposes of these group sessions are to give participants an opportunity to—
- Develop problem-solving skills.
- Present their small group decisions to the total group for evaluation.
- Interact with their peers.

Course Evaluation

Appendix G contains an example of a Participant Course Evaluation. This evaluation, or a similar one used by your local Red Cross unit, should be given to participants before they leave the class to find out how they felt about the course. Appendix H contains an Instructor Course Evaluation. This evaluation asks your opinion about the course materials. You should fill out this form the **first** and **fourth** times that you teach this course. The form should be returned directly to the national headquarters of the American Red Cross. (The address is on the evaluation.) The information will help evaluate how well the course materials work for both new and experienced instructors.

Evaluation of Participants

It is important to know how much the participants have learned. In order to receive a course completion certificate, participants must pass all the skills tests and pass a written examination.

Written Examination

The written examination is given after the participants have completed all the skills checkouts. **A participant should not take the written examination unless he or she has passed all the skills tests for each session.** Check that each participant has passed all the skills checkouts before giving him or her the written examination. If you have used the *Lifeguarding Skills Checklist* (Appendix D), you will be able to check this quickly.

Sixty test questions, divided into groups, are provided in Appendix I of this manual. The instructor should create a 40-question examination by choosing a specified number of questions from each group. Appendix I also includes an answer sheet to be copied and handed out to each participant with the examination, and an answer key giving the answers for all 60 questions. **Other**

written examinations should not be substituted for the test questions provided since the questions test the major objectives of the course.

Participants should not refer to their textbooks or *Supplements* when taking the examination.

The passing grade for each written test is 80 percent (32 questions correct out of 40). If a participant does not answer the minimum number of questions correctly, he or she should be directed to read the relevant section of the textbook or the *Supplement.* Educational research suggests that encouraging students to review their understanding of facts and concepts in context (by referring to the complete unit rather than by referring to the appropriate sentence) is more likely to encourage long-term retention of the information.

Avoid reviewing the answers to individual test questions with participants. The purpose of the tests in this manual is to ascertain which participants have mastered the content of the course. The questions on these tests represent only a small sample of all the questions that might be asked. When a participant answers a particular question incorrectly, he or she may not understand the broader objective that the question addresses. In providing participants with feedback on their test performance, you should stress the broader objective and not the specific question. An example of a broad objective is: "To ensure that participants learn the factors in pool maintenance and the responsibility of the lifeguard in regard to them."

Participants who pass the test may be told content areas for questions they missed; for example, you might say, "The question you answered incorrectly was about rescue breathing in shallow water."

If a participant has difficulty reading, you may test the participant by reading the questions aloud. Since this should be done without disturbing the other participants, oral tests should not be administered until all other participants have completed the written test. You may need to schedule additional time for oral tests.

Note: Participants must be told that they must pass a final skills test and pass a written examination with a score of 80 percent or better. Some timed events and physical conditioning are a required part of the course, and some of the final skills tests are timed. Due to water temperature and weather conditions, the times given in this manual for timed swims and exit requirements may need to be adjusted for open water facilities. Participants should possess the strength, stamina, and ability to perform the skills commensurate with the course requirements.

Test Security

Test security is your responsibility. Participants must not be allowed to see the written examination before it is handed out. If the examination and answer sheets routinely become available to participants before class, the examination results will be worthless in determining which participants understand the course material.

You should collect both the answer sheets and the examinations from the participants after they have completed the examination. **Do not return the answer sheets to the participants.** Developing and validating good tests is expensive. To safeguard the effectiveness of these tests, it is essential that you collect all copies of the examination and the answer sheets when the examination is completed.

Participants who successfully demonstrate all the skills, and pass the final skills tests, and the written examination will receive course completion certificates.

Criteria for Grading Participants

The *Course Record* (Form 6418) requires that you enter a grade of pass, fail, or incomplete for each participant. The information below will help you assign the correct grade:

- Pass (P)

  "Pass" (P) should be entered as the final grade for a participant who has passed all the skill checkouts and scored at least 80 percent on the written examination. If the participant passes all the skill checkouts but fails the written examination, you may create an alternate version of the exam by substituting the 10 unused questions for 10 of the questions you chose initially. You may give the test orally if you think that the participant's score on the written test was low because of poor reading ability. In this case, enter each answer on the answer sheet and score the test as usual. If the participant scores at least 80 percent on the retest, "Pass" (P) should be entered as the final grade.

- Fail (F)

  "Fail" (F) should be entered as the final grade for a participant who has not passed **all** the required skills and/or the written examination and prefers not to be retested, or who does not pass a retest.

- Incomplete (Inc)   "Incomplete" (Inc) should be entered as the final grade if the participant is unable to complete the course due to certain circumstances, such as illness or a death in the family. An "incomplete" is given only when arrangements to complete the training have been made.

Skills Tests

To successfully complete the Lifeguard Training course, a participant must pass all the skills tests described in Sessions 9 and 10. Appendix J is a Final Skills Checklist for the instructor to use in checking off each participant as he or she passes each final skill test.

List of Equipment and Supplies

Following is a list of the equipment and supplies needed to teach the American Red Cross Lifeguard Training course. A checklist of equipment and supplies is provided in Appendix B.

Required Materials for Participants
American Red Cross Lifeguard Training textbook
    (Stock No. 321119)
American Red Cross Lifeguard Training Supplement
    (Stock No. 329448)
A notebook and a pen or pencil
A bathing suit and a towel (for every session)
A face mask, swim fins, and a snorkel (Not all participants may be able to provide this equipment. Instructors may have to work out sharing arrangements or rent equipment from scuba diving shops. Some facilities may be able to provide certain items.)

Equipment Required for the Course
(The number in parentheses after each item indicates the number required for a class of 10 participants.)
American Red Cross Lifeguard Training textbook (10)
American Red Cross Lifeguard Training Supplement (10)
Lifeguard Training Course Written Tests and Answer Sheets (10)
Shepherd's crook or reaching pole (2)
Heaving line (2)
Ring buoy, heaving jug, or throw bag (2)

Backboard and set of (6 each) straps or ties (2)
Blanket (for backboard head collar) (2)
Padding material (2 towels each) for backboard (2)
Rigid cervical collar (2)
Whistle (1)
Set of 3 signal flags (1)
Diving brick (2)
Personal flotation devices (PFDs) (2)
Rescue board or surfboard (2)
Scuba weight belt, without weights (2)
Stopwatch (minimum of 2 for final skills test)

Additional Equipment Required for Course at Waterfront Facility
Rescue boat(s) and oars, or canoe(s) and paddles

Additional Equipment Required for Course at Swimming Pool
Kits for testing chemical balance of water

Suggested Instructional Aids
16mm projector, screen, extension cord, take-up reel, and spare
    bulbs, or VHS-VCR and monitor
Extra paper and pencils
Chalkboard and chalk or similar items (such as flip chart with easel
    and marking pens)
List of rules and regulations, various emergency action plans, and
    records and reports from local aquatic facilities

Suggested Audiovisuals

Red Cross Audiovisuals
All audiovisuals are shown at the option of the instructor. The time
required to show audiovisuals can be compensated for in each
session by the reduced amount of time then required for discussion
and demonstration. Appropriate audiovisuals are listed for each
session.

A 60-minute audiovisual, *Emergency Aquatic Skills* (Stock No.
329331), covers the following subjects. Times are rounded up to the
nearest minute.

Unit 1—*Introduction to the Program,* 3 minutes
Unit 2—*Recognition of Drowning Victim,* 2 minutes
Unit 3—*Nonswimming Assists,* 7 minutes
Unit 4—*Entries,* 7 minutes

Unit 5—*Approaches,* 4 minutes
Unit 6—*Swimming Assists and Tows,* 8 minutes
Unit 7—*Removal From the Water,* 9 minutes
Unit 8—*Defenses and Escapes,* 9 minutes
Unit 9—*Advanced Rescue Skills,* 15 minutes
Unit 10—*Review and Closing,* 3 minutes
Appendix C is a Video Calibration Chart that enables the instructor
to locate specific segments of the video. A separate audiovisual,
Spinal Injury Management (Stock No. 329328) (approximately 25
minutes), covers procedures and techniques for managing suspected
or identified spinal injuries.

Other American Red Cross audiovisuals that are appropriate for
the Lifeguard Training course are the following:
- *Snorkeling Skills and Rescue Techniques* (Stock No. 321648),
  approximately 13 minutes
- *Preventive Lifeguarding* (Stock No. 321655), approximately 10
  minutes

Audiovisuals From Other Sources
- *Drowning: Facts and Myths*
  (1977) 10 minutes
- *On Drowning*
  (1970) 17 minutes
- *The Reason People Drown*
  (1988) 25 minutes

Available for purchase from:
Water Safety Film, Inc.
3 Boulder Brae Lane
Larchmont, NY 10538
(914) 834-7536

- *The Drowning Machine*
  (1981) 20 minutes

Available for purchase from:
Hornbein Productions
740 Elmwood St.
State College, PA 16801
(814) 234-7886

Instructor References

- *American Red Cross: Adult CPR Workbook* (Stock No. 329128)
- *American Red Cross: CPR Workbook* (Stock No. 329364)
- *American Red Cross CPR Instructor's Manual* (Stock No. 329367)
- *American Red Cross CPR: Basic Life Support for the Professional Rescuer* (Stock No. 329365)
- *American Red Cross CPR Instructor's Manual Supplement: Basic Life Support for the Professional Rescuer* (Stock No. 329368)
- *American Red Cross: Basic Water Safety Textbook* (Stock No. 329312)
- *American Red Cross: Emergency Water Safety Textbook* (Stock No. 329313)
- *Basic Water Safety and Emergency Water Safety Instructor's Manual* (Stock No. 329314)
- *Lifeguard Training* (Stock No. 321119)
- *Lifeguard Training Supplement* (Stock No. 329448)
- *American Red Cross: Standard First Aid Workbook* (Stock No. 329380)
- *American Red Cross: Standard First Aid Instructor's Manual* (Stock No. 329381)
- *American Red Cross Rescue Breathing and Choking Supplement* (Stock No. 329286)
- *Introduction to Health Services Education* (Stock No. 321252)

Lifeguard Training Course Outline

Session 1

Activity	Approximate Time
Course Introduction	10 minutes
Preface	5 minutes
Philosophy of Lifeguarding	5 minutes
Characteristics, Knowledge, Personal Skills, and Responsibilities of Lifeguards	10 minutes
Course Benefits and Requirements	5 minutes

Preventive Lifeguarding
    Rules and Regulations
    Enforcement of Rules
    Facility Capacities
    Supervising Bathers—Facility Tour
	35 minutes

Victim Recognition	10 minutes
Break	10 minutes
Skills Screening	40 minutes

Skills Practice
    Reaching Assists
    Equipment Extension
    Throwing Assists
	40 minutes
	    (10 minutes)
	    (10 minutes)
	    (20 minutes)

Review and Assignment	5 minutes
Counseling	5 minutes

Session 1, Total Time   3 hours

Session 2

Activity	Approximate Time
Review	5 minutes

Selection and Training
    Pre-employment Orientation
    In-Service Training
	25 minutes

Emergency Classifications	15 minutes
Break	10 minutes

Skills Practice
    Entries
    Approach Stroking and Ready Position
    Rescue Kicks
    Surface Diving and Underwater Swimming
    Recovery of a Submerged Victim
	105 minutes
	(35 minutes)
	(15 minutes)
	(20 minutes)
	(25 minutes)
	(10 minutes)

Conditioning Swim	10 minutes
Review and Assignment	5 minutes

Session 2 Total Time   **2 hours, 55 minutes**

Session 3

Activity	Approximate Time
Review	5 minutes
Communication Systems	15 minutes
Break	10 minutes

Skills Practice
    Swimming Approaches
    Swimming Assists
    Tows and Carries
	110 minutes
	(5 minutes)
	(15 minutes)
	(50 minutes)

Conditioning Swim	15 minutes
Review and Assignment	5 minutes
Session 3, Total Time	**2 hours, 40 minutes**

Session 4

Activity	Approximate Time
Review	5 minutes
Health and Sanitation	10 minutes
Swimming Pool Maintenance	20 minutes
Emergency Action Plans	25 minutes
Special Assignment	15 minutes
Break	10 minutes
Skills Practice	75 minutes
Removing a Victim from the Water:	
Lifts, Assists, and Carries	(15 minutes)
Defense	(10 minutes)
Escapes	(35 minutes)
Multiple Near-Drowning Maneuver	(15 minutes)
Conditioning Swim	15 minutes
Review and Assignment	5 minutes

Session 4, Total Time   **3 hours**

Session 5

Activity	Approximate Time
Review	5 minutes

Special Situations
    Hypothermia
    Heat Emergencies
    Seizures
	40 minutes

Rescue Equipment	5 minutes
Break	10 minutes
Skills Practice Using Rescue Equipment	80 minutes
Conditioning Swim	25 minutes
Review	5 minutes
Session 5, Total Time	**2 hours, 50 minutes**

Session 6

Activity	Approximate Time
Review	5 minutes
Records and Reports	30 minutes
Personal and Safety Equipment	10 minutes
Break	10 minutes

Skills Practice
    Rescue Breathing
    Rescue Equipment and Rescue Breathing
	90 minutes
	(30 minutes)
	(60 minutes)

Conditioning Swim	20 minutes
Review and Assignment	5 minutes
Session 6, Total Time	**2 hours, 50 minutes**

Session 7

Activity	Approximate Time
Review	5 minutes
Spinal Injuries	30 minutes
Audiovisual—*Spinal Injury Mangement* (optional but strongly recommended; not counted in total time)	25 minutes*
Break	10 minutes
Skills Practice Spinal Injury, Shallow Water Spinal Injury, Deep Water	100 minutes (70 minutes) (30 minutes)
Conditioning Swim	20 minutes
Review and Assignment	5 minutes
Session 7, Total Time	**2 hours, 50 minutes**

* optional

Session 8

Activity	Approximate Time
Review	5 minutes
Search and Recovery Equipment and Operations	20 minutes
Weather and Environmental Conditions	10 minutes
Waterfront Areas	20 minutes
Break	10 minutes
Skills Practice	95 minutes
Mask, Fins, and Snorkel	(35 minutes)
Entering the Water Wearing Snorkeling Equipment	(20 minutes)
Swimming Wearing Snorkeling Equipment	(15 minutes)
Search and Recovery Operations	(15 minutes)
Rescue of a Scuba Diver	(10 minutes)
Rescue Boats (optional and not counted in total time)	(15 minutes)*
Conditioning Swim	15 minutes
Review and Assignment	5 minutes

Session 8, Total Time   2 hours, 55 minutes

* optional

Session 9

Activity	Approximate Time
Review	30 minutes
Written Examination	40 minutes
Break	10 minutes
Skills Tests	60 minutes
Assignment	5 minutes
Session 9, Total Time	**2 hours, 25 minutes**

Session 10

Activity	Approximate Time
Review of Written Examination	15 minutes
Final Skills Tests	60 minutes
Review and Summary	20 minutes
Session 10, Total Time	**1 hour, 35 minutes**

Total Time for course   **27 hours**

Session 1

Time	Approximately 3 hours
Topics	Course Introduction and Welcome; Philosophy of Lifeguarding; Characteristics, Knowledge, Personal Skills, and Responsibilities of Lifeguards; Course Benefits and Requirements; Preventive Lifeguarding; Victim Recognition; Skills Screening; Counseling; Nonswimming and Equipment Assists
References	Textbook: Preface; Chapters 1, 2, and 4; Chapter 9, pages 9-1 and 9-2; Appendix A *Supplement:* Chapter 1, pages 2 through 9 *Note:* All page references for the textbook refer to the 1983, 1984 edition.
Materials and Equipment	Chalkboard and chalk, or flip chart and markers; pencils and notebooks; shepherd's crook or reaching pole; heaving line; ring buoy; throw bag; appropriate audiovisual equipment (optional)
Facilities	Classroom and a pool or lake
Suggested Audiovisual	*Emergency Aquatic Skills:* Unit 1—*Introduction to the Program,* 3 minutes; Unit 2—*Recognition of Drowning Victim,* 2 minutes; Unit 3—*Nonswimming Assists,* 7 minutes

Course Introduction—Welcome

Suggested Time	10 minutes

Objective   To familiarize prospective participants with the course content and design and to introduce yourself and any assistant instructors and aides

Activity   Welcome prospective participants. Discuss the following course objectives:
- To ensure that participants become aware of and recognize the common hazards associated with various types of aquatic facilities and develop the knowledge and skills to eliminate or minimize such hazards
- To ensure that participants develop the skills necessary to recognize a person in a distress or drowning situation and to rescue that person
- To ensure that participants understand the lifeguard-employer and lifeguard-patron relationships
- To establish an awareness of the responsibilities of a lifeguard and instill an enthusiasm for carrying them out
- To develop participants' speed, endurance, and technique in swimming and lifeguarding skills

Explain the course requirements:
- Total hours.
- Meeting times and breaks.
- Facility regulations.
- Attendance requirements. Point out that participants must attend all sessions to be eligible for certification.
- Entry skills requirements.
- Reading assignments. Explain that they will be using two books: the *Lifeguard Training* textbook and the *Lifeguard Training Supplement,* which provides updated material as well as content and skills previously taught in the Red Cross Lifesaving course.

- Discussions and participant participation.
- Evaluation and grading.
- Written examination. Participants must answer 80 percent of the questions correctly in order to pass.
- Final skills test.
- Safety of participants, and facility rules and regulations.
- Current certificates—An American Red Cross Standard First Aid certificate (or equivalent) and an American Red Cross Adult CPR certificate (or equivalent) must be obtained prior to taking the course or before graduating from it.

Preface to the Lifeguard Training Textbook

Suggested Time   5 minutes

Objective   To familiarize participants with the Red Cross commitment to lifeguard training

Activity   Participants should be aware of the extent of Red Cross involvement in and commitment to the training of lifeguards.

Refer participants to the Preface in the textbook. Briefly discuss the growth of the Red Cross water safety program and the Red Cross involvement in lifeguard training.

Philosophy of Lifeguarding

Suggested Time   5 minutes

Objective   To make participants aware of the Red Cross philosophy of lifeguarding

Suggested   *Emergency Aquatic Skills:* Unit 1—

Audiovisual *Introduction to the Program,* 3 minutes

Activity Refer participants to the textbook, pages 1-1 and 1-2.

Emphasize to the participants that the primary concern of the lifeguard is the safety of others.

Discuss the need for lifeguards to have training and knowledge in recognizing potential hazards, preventing accidents and injuries, making swimming rescues, and in the other duties expected of them and discussed on page 1-2.

Stress that Lifeguard Training is a basic training course and that participants should continue to receive additional training at their place of employment.

Characteristics, Knowledge, Personal Skills, and Responsibilities of Lifeguards

Suggested Time 10 minutes

Objective

Personal Characteristics
To make participants aware of the personal characteristics required of lifeguards

Activity Refer participants to the textbook, page 2-1. Briefly discuss the importance of the following characteristics of lifeguards. These points should be emphasized throughout the course.
- Reliability—A lifeguard should be punctual, assume responsibilities, and accept assignments.
- Emotional stability—A lifeguard must work well under pressure.
- Tact and judgment—A lifeguard should have the respect and cooperation of patrons and be courteous when enforcing the rules.

- Physical fitness—A lifeguard must always maintain a proper level of physical fitness.
- Positive attitude—A lifeguard should work well with others and follow all rules and regulations.

Knowledge

Objective

To increase participants' awareness of the knowledge required of a lifeguard

Activity

Refer participants to the textbook, page 2-2.
Point out that most of the following subjects will be covered in more depth during the course:
- Rules and regulations—Lifeguards must know the rules and regulations of the facility where they are employed. They must obey the rules.
- Facility characteristics—Lifeguards must be thoroughly familiar with the hazards and emergencies that may occur at the facility. Limit any discussion at this time to the need for knowledge rather than specific characteristics or conditions.
- Chain of command—Refer participants to Appendix A in the textbook. Select two common types of chains of command, one simple (such as a small town), one more complex (such as a recreation department, large city, or camp). Point out the lifeguard's position in the chain of command in each.
- Additional duties—Lifeguards should understand that any additional duties, such as maintenance or instruction, must not interfere with the supervision of bathers.
- Legal responsibilities—Limit the discussion of legal responsibilities to the lifeguard's obligation to the patrons, to his or her employer, and to himself or herself.

Note: Further discussion on liability must only be held by the legal counsel for the facility where the lifeguard will be working or by the lifeguard's personal attorney.

Personal Skills

Objective

To reemphasize participants' need for additional training

Activity

Refer participants to the textbook, pages 2-2 and 2-3.

Emphasize the benefits of skill practice and development. Discuss the following areas of skill development:

- Swimming and rescue skills—Lifeguards need to develop speed and endurance.
- Use of equipment—Lifeguards must be skilled in the use of rescue equipment; such as rescue buoys or backboards; communications equipment, such as whistles and flags; and maintenance equipment, such as filters or vacuums.
- First aid—Lifeguards must be able to relate skills learned in a first aid course to the accidents and injuries common to aquatic facilities.
- CPR—Lifeguards must be aware of the necessity for training and practice in CPR skills.

Responsibilities

Objective

To create an awareness of the job responsibilities of lifeguards and to advise participants of their limits of authority.

Activity

Refer participants to the textbook, pages 2-3 and 2-4.

Discuss the primary and secondary responsibilities of lifeguards. Have participants identify the limits of responsibility for various positions in the chain of command (refer participants to Appendix A).

Remind participants that the safety of bathers is the lifeguard's primary responsibility and never takes a secondary position to any other duties.

Course Benefits and Requirements

Suggested Time   5 minutes

Objective   To ensure that participants understand both the benefits and requirements of the course

Activity   Briefly discuss with participants the personal benefits of lifeguarding, such as physical development and the development of public relations skills and teamwork.

Explain that the course will require extensive physical activity. There will be conditioning swims during the course, but participants will need to do additional conditioning outside of class.

Explain that the final test will contain both skills testing and distance and timed events and that participants will have to achieve a score of 80 percent or better on the written examination.

Emphasize that participants who have any physical limitations should inform the instructor. Participants who have physical limitations that could endanger themselves or others during the course should not be allowed to continue.

Preventive Lifeguarding

Suggested Time   35 minutes

Objective

Rules and Regulations
To develop participants' understanding of the need for the establishment of certain rules and regulations

Activity
Emphasize that lifeguards are governed not only by staff rules but also by the rules that apply to the patrons.

Refer participants to the textbook, pages 4-1 through 4-3.

Discuss briefly with participants the need for educating the patrons of an aquatic facility about its rules and regulations.

Ask participants for examples of rules and regulations from each of the following categories:
- Personal conduct (running, pushing, diving)
- Use of equipment (diving boards, slides, rescue equipment)
- Local ordinances (showers, food, drinks)

Objective

Enforcement of Rules
To increase participants' awareness of the different methods of enforcing rules at an aquatic facility

Activity
Refer participants to the textbook, pages 4-3 and 4-4.

Briefly discuss enforcement procedures for various rules and regulations. Review the limits of authority for individual positions in the chain of command. (Refer participants to Appendix A.)

Objective

Facility Capacities
To introduce participants to methods of establishing safety capacity limits

Activity

Refer participants to the textbook, pages 4-4 and 4-5.

Discuss the different formulas used to establish capacity limits for aquatic facilities:
- Patron capacity—Consider the size and shape of the facility.
- Lifeguard-to-patron ratio—Consider the size and shape of the facility, the type of facility, and the activities that occur.

Note: Refer to local and/or state regulations.

Objective

Supervision of Bathers—Facility Tour
To familiarize participants with the various methods of supervision used at aquatic facilities and to increase the knowledge of procedures used to ensure bather safety

Activity

Refer participants to the textbook, pages 4-5 to 4-18. Tour the facility, using the text material as a guide when appropriate.
- Facility sections—Explain the purposes for dividing a facility into sections for various activities, such as swimming, diving, and instruction.
- Areas of responsibility—Discuss the factors to be considered when setting up areas of responsibility, such as the size and shape of the facility, the number of bathers, and environmental conditions.
- Visual surveillance—Discuss the proper method of scanning an assigned area of responsibility, i.e., continually scanning back and forth across the entire area. Point out the blind spot directly in front of and below the lifeguard stand.
- Zone coverage and total coverage—Discuss the advantages and disadvantages of—

31

1. Zone coverage.
   Advantages—concentration on limited area and double coverage
   Disadvantages—more staff required for large facilities, confusion in overlap areas, failure to scan entire area
2. Total coverage.
   Advantage—requires small number of staff members
   Disadvantages—areas may be too large, guards have a tendency to watch extreme boundaries too much of the time

- Back-up coverage—Explain the purposes of back-up coverage—safety and continuous supervision. Discuss the different systems for back-up coverage.

Have participants take positions at different stations to help illustrate area limits and blind spots.

- Safety checks and buddy systems—Discuss the value of safety checks and buddy systems and the methods of establishing them at different aquatic facilities.
- Lifeguard stations—Explain the factors used to determine the location of lifeguard stations, such as the size and shape of the facility, water depth, the number of patrons, and environmental conditions. Discuss the advantages and disadvantages of the following types of lifeguard stations:
  —Elevated stations (better field of vision versus injury potential when getting down in a hurry for an emergency)
  —Ground level stations (closer proximity to patrons versus a more limited field of vision)
  —Boat stations (closer to swimmers at outer edges of swimming area versus

the need to maneuver the boat and the
distance to shore)
- Rotating and relieving lifeguards—Briefly
  explain the need for rotations and relief
  breaks. Point out the advantages and
  disadvantages of different procedures for
  various facilities.
- Practice relieving a lifeguard at a stand,
  maintaining constant surveillance of the
  pool or other swimming area.

Discuss the following material:
- Accident charts and contour depth lines—
  Discuss the use of accident charts and
  contour depth lines as preventive
  measures to ensure the safety of bathers.
  Demonstrate the use of an accident chart.
  Explain how to construct a contour depth
  line at an aquatic facility.
- Hazardous areas—Briefly identify and
  discuss the hazardous areas that may
  be found at an aquatic facility. Ask
  participants for recommendations on
  how to minimize or eliminate hazards.

Victim Recognition

**Suggested
Time**   10 minutes

**Suggested
Audiovisual**   *Emergency Aquatic Skills:* Unit 2—*Recognition
                of a Drowning Victim,* 2 minutes, Unit 3—
                Nonswimming Assists, 7 minutes

                Note: If Unit 3 is not shown, the time needed
                for skills practice may be longer than
                indicated

Objective   To enable participants to recognize the signs
                that indicate a drowning victim and to

distinguish between a drowning victim and a distressed victim

Activity

Refer participants to the textbook, pages 9-1 and 9-2.

Discuss the distinguishing features of the following situations:

- Distress situation—The victim may be attempting to swim but is making no progress. The victim may be able to wave his or her arms and to call for help. This victim may easily become a panicky and active drowning victim. The lifeguard must be cautious in approaching this victim.
- Drowning situation—The victim is unable to call for help or to wave his or her arms.
  —The **passive** victim may suddenly slip underwater. A passive situation could be caused by a heart attack, a stroke, being hit by an object, hyperventilation, cold water shock, alcohol, or drugs.
  —The **active** victim's arms are extended to the side, thrashing water in a vertical movement. There is no forward progress. The victim alternately raises and lowers himself or herself in the water and is unable to call for help.

Break

Suggested Time

10 minutes

Activity

Participants should change clothes and prepare for the in-water skills practice.

Skills Screening

Suggested Time   40 minutes

Objective   To evaluate participants' present skills and endurance level for swimming and lifeguarding

Activity   Test each participant on each of the following skills. To be allowed to continue in the course, participants must be able to demonstrate each skill satisfactorily.

1. Swim 500 yards continuously using each of the following strokes for at least 50 yards each: crawl, breaststroke, elementary backstroke, sidestroke.
2. Surface dive to a minimum depth of 9 feet and bring a 10-pound diving brick to the surface.
3. Surface dive to a minimum depth of 5 feet and swim underwater a minimum of 15 yards.
4. Tread water for one minute.

Skills Practice: Reaching Assists, Equipment Extension, Throwing Assists

Objective   To ensure participants can demonstrate the ability to make safe and effective nonswimming assists using arm, leg, or body extension, and equipment

Reaching Assists

Suggested Time

10 minutes

Activity

Refer participants to pages 2 through 9 in the *Supplement*. Discuss, demonstrate, and practice the proper technique for making reaching assists using arm, leg, or body extension.

Emphasize the typical lifeguarding situations in which to use these rescues and reinforce the following techniques and procedures:

- Lie flat on deck or dock with body firmly anchored. Grasp victim's wrist from above and pull slowly and carefully.
- If standing in water, brace feet and lean back when reaching, while holding onto a support. If victim is beyond reach, extend a leg. Have a firm grasp on a pool ladder, overflow trough, piling, or other stationary object.
- Grasp victim as soon as possible.
- Keep talking to victim to calm and instruct him or her.

Equipment Extension

Suggested Time

10 minutes

Activity

Discuss, demonstrate, and practice the following equipment extension techniques using a shepherd's crook and/or reaching pole, or rescue equipment such as a kickboard.

Standing on Shore, Deck, or Pier

- With an unconscious victim, carefully position hook end of shepherd's crook around victim's chest, under the armpits.

36

- While firmly braced, slowly pull the victim to safety with a hand-over-hand technique.
- Grasp victim as soon as possible.
- Brace feet.
- With an active victim, gently extend rounded hook end of shepherd's crook to victim's chest, allowing victim to grasp it, or extend the crook past the victim with the open side of hook opposite victim.
- When pole contacts victim, turn it so that the open side encircles victim's body.

Wading Assists
- Wade into water no more than chest deep.
- Lean back before reaching out to victim.
- Lifeguard can extend pole or shepherd's crook, or free-floating support such as a buoyant cushion, PFD, or a kickboard to the victim.

Throwing Assists

Suggested Time

20 minutes

Activity

Discuss and demonstrate the kinds of rescue equipment described in the *Supplement* and practice both the general technique of throwing rescue equipment and any necessary additional techniques for specific equipment.

General Throwing Technique
- Stand so you will maintain balance and bend knees.
- Hold coiled line over palm of nonthrowing hand so that hand is open, flat, and extended towards victim.
- Step on nonthrowing end of the rope.
- Extend foot opposite throwing arm.
- Release rope or equipment at eye level. Throw with an underhand toss and follow through with throwing arm.
- Throw the rope and rescue device over victim's shoulder and beyond victim but within reach.

- Throw the rope upwind or upstream so that the drift will bring rope and/or device within victim's reach.
- Retrieve victim quickly and smoothly using a steady pull.
- Recoil the rope as you pull victim in, in case victim lets go and you have to throw again.

Rescue Devices
- Ring Buoy and Line
  — Step on end of line in front of the "lemon," with foot opposite the throwing hand placed forward before throwing.
  — Grasp ring buoy with throwing hand, fingers holding the underside of the buoy.
  (If wind keeps buoy out of victim's reach and no other flotation device is available, swim out with buoy. When buoy is within victim's reach, push buoy to victim, keeping it between yourself and victim.)
  — After victim has firm grasp on buoy, tow victim to safety, grasping line well out of victim's reach. Talk to victim to calm and instruct him or her.
- Heaving Line
  — Step on one end of line to prevent throwing rope into the water.
  — Slip one-half of the coil in each hand to give sufficient weight to coil in throwing hand to throw it accurately.
  — Attach a buoyant weight to the end of the rope for better throwing accuracy.
- Heaving Jug (demonstrate only)
  — Note that it is suitable for home pools.
  — Place foot opposite throwing arm on end of line.
  — Throw by grasping handle of jug and releasing at forward end of swing.
- Throw Bag (describe only)

— Rope should be stored in bag so that it uncoils easily when bag is thrown, and drawstring at top of bag should be sufficiently loose to allow rope to leave bag.
— Grasp bag by the top and throw underhand while holding one end of line in nonthrowing hand.

Review and Assignment

Suggested Time
5 minutes

Objective:
To ensure participants' understanding of the information covered during this session

Activity
Review the session's main subjects with the participants. Answer any questions participants may have.
Give the following reading assignment:
• Textbook: Chapter 3; Chapter 5, pages 5-1 through 5-10; and Appendixes A and B
• *Supplement:* Chapter 1, pages 15 through 21; Chapter 3, pages 34 and 35

Counseling

Suggested Time
5 minutes

Objective
To provide individual evaluations of skills for those whose skills are weak or unacceptable

Activity
Advise any participants with unacceptable skills that it is not advisable to continue in the course. Discuss weaknesses and suggest methods of skills improvement.

Session 2

Time	Approximately 3 hours
Topics	Selection and Training; Emergency Classifications; Entries; Approach Stroking; Ready Position; Rescue Kicks; Surface Diving and Underwater Swimming
References	Textbook: Chapter 3; Chapter 5, pages 5–1 through 5–10; and Appendixes A and B *Supplement* : Chapter 1, pages 15 through 21; Chapter 3, pages 34 and 35
Materials and Equipment	Chalkboard and chalk, or flip chart and markers; appropriate audiovisual equipment (optional)
Facilities	Classroom and a pool or lake
Suggested Audiovisual	*Emergency Aquatic Skills,* Unit 4—*Entries* , 7 minutes

Review

Suggested Time	5 minutes
Objective	To verify participants' understanding of the information covered in the previous session
Activity	Review the key subjects and objectives of the preceding session. Answer any questions participants may have.

Selection and Training

Suggested Time

25 minutes

Objective

To increase participants' awareness of the training requirements for lifeguards

Objective

Preemployment

To increase participants' awareness of the preemployment requirements for lifeguards

Activity

Refer participants to the textbook, pages 3-1 to 3-3.

Briefly discuss the need for the following examinations and training required for individuals seeking a lifeguard position.

- Physical examination—All lifeguard candidates should submit the results of a physical examination certifying that they are able to perform the duties of a lifeguard.
- Lifeguarding training—Candidates for a lifeguard position should possess a current lifeguarding certificate from a certifying organization, such as the American Red Cross.
- Swimming skills—The candidate must possess the physical skills and stamina needed to assist others in the water.
- First aid skills—Participants must either have a current American Red Cross Standard First Aid certificate (or equivalent) or earn one before they graduate from the Lifeguard Training course.
- CPR—CPR is taught as part of the Standard First Aid course. Participants must have a current American Red Cross CPR certificate (or equivalent) or earn one before they graduate from the course.
- Small craft skills—Use of small craft in rescues will be briefly discussed and

demonstrated in Session 8, but not practiced unless the instructor opts to do so.

Orientation (Preservice Training)

Objective
To advise participants of the information needed for a thorough orientation to a facility's operations

Activity
Refer participants to the textbook, pages 3-3 and 3-4, and Appendix A.

Point out the need for lifeguards to be thoroughly familiar with the total operations of the facility where they will be working.

Briefly discuss each of the following subjects and how they relate to the lifeguard's responsibilities:

- Management—Refer participants to Appendix A.
- Operation of facility—Discuss the lifeguard's role in the smooth operation of an aquatic facility. Stress the importance of fulfilling job responsibilities, such as maintenance, and following the daily schedule.
- Rules and regulations—Remind participants of the importance of rules and regulations that pertain to lifeguard conduct.
- Preventive lifeguarding—Discuss the need for orientations on subjects such as hazardous areas, rotation methods for lifeguards, and procedures for foul weather.
- Records and reports—Point out the need for lifeguards to be familiar with all records and reports required at the facility. Refer participants to sample record and report forms in Appendix B in the textbook.
- Legal responsibility—Emphasize that all discussions of liability and legal responsibility should be conducted by the

facility's legal counsel. This will ensure that there are no misunderstandings and that all lifeguards receive the same information.

- Emergency procedures—Explain that orientations must include an explanation of all emergency procedures for the facility.

In-Service Training

Objective

To provide participants with additional information on the need for in-service training

Activity

Refer participants to the textbook, pages 3-5 to 3-9.

Discuss with participants the following benefits of an in-service training program:

- Increased mental alertness and physical conditioning
- Increased ability to react to emergencies in a positive manner

Point out the need for an in-service training program that is tailor-made to the facility. Ways in which facilities may vary are—

- Pool filtration and chemical balance.
- Beach configuration and strength of currents.
- Hazardous areas.
- Size and shape.

Explain scheduling procedures for training sessions.

Briefly discuss each of the following subjects in order to increase the participants' understanding of overall training and conditioning for lifeguards:

- Physical training and conditioning— Emphasize general conditioning of the cardiovascular system, muscular strength, endurance, and flexibility. Specific conditioning incorporates endurance and muscular strength with swimming and lifeguarding skills.

- Fitness testing—Discuss the following advantages of timed tests and performance standards:
  — They are objective. Examiner does not have to rely solely on experience.
  — They provide meaningful feedback to lifeguards.
  — They provide a tangible goal for lifeguards.

The results of fitness testing should be recorded.

Note: Briefly discuss the suggested training outline in the textbook, pages 3-7 to 3-9. Point out that some of the tests described may not be applicable to certain facilities or may need to be modified. Explain that some of the "Lifesaving Events" described on pages 3-7 and 3-8 in the textbook will be described or taught using the techniques given in the *Supplement* and that some different terminology will be used. Remind participants, for example, that artificial respiration and mouth-to-mouth resuscitation are now generally referred to as rescue breathing.

Emergency Classifications

Suggested Time   15 minutes

Objective   To enable participants to identify and recognize the various types of emergencies that may occur at an aquatic facility

Activity   Refer participants to the textbook, pages 5-1 and 5-2.
Explain the two classifications of emergencies.

45

Life-Threatening

These emergencies require immediate action by the lifeguard to prevent loss of life or further injury. This category includes—
- Stopped breathing.
- Severe bleeding.
- Poisoning.
- Spinal injuries.
- Heart attack.

Non-Life-Threatening

These emergencies require action by the lifeguard. Danger to the victim is minimal. There are two types:
1. Major—Such as broken bones, seizures out of the water, or a tired swimmer.
2. Minor—Such as sunburn or abrasions.

Suggested Audiovisual   *Emergency Aquatic Skills:* Unit 4—*Entries,* 7 minutes

Break

Suggested Time   10 minutes

Activity   Participants should change clothes and prepare for the in-water skills practice.

Skills Practice: Entries, Approach Stroking and Ready Position, Rescue Kicks, Surface Diving and Underwater Swimming

Entries

Suggested Time   35 minutes

Objective   To ensure that participants can demonstrate techniques for entries into the water that provide safety for the rescuer and maximum visual contact with the victim.

Refer participants to pages 15 through 21 in the *Supplement.*

Discuss the factors that help determine the type of entry to use. These factors include—
- Depth of water.
- Entry height.
- Water clarity.
- Knowledge of bottom conditions.
- Distance to victim.
- Stress level of victim.

Activity   Explain, demonstrate, and practice the following entries:

Stride Jump
- Water should be at least 5 feet deep.
- Entry height of not more than 3 feet.
- Leap outward with legs in stride or scissors-kick position.
- Arms fully extended behind, to the side, or crossed on the chest, body leaning forward at a 45-degree angle.
- Eyes on the victim.
- Squeeze or scissor legs together upon entry to provide upward thrust.
- If arms extended or to side, pull hands forward and down upon entry. If arms in front of chest, press hands down and move outward in breaststroke fashion.

Feetfirst Entry From a Height
- Do not attempt in unknown water depth.
- Use when entering from height of more than 3 feet.
- Enter in vertical position.
- Arms at sides.
- Legs together, knees slightly flexed.
- Head erect, eyes on victim.

- Slow descent after head enters by extending arms outwards and spreading legs in scissors or breaststroke position.
- Swim to surface.

Ease-In Entry
- Use in conjunction with victim of suspected spinal injury, or when water is less than 5 feet deep, or water depth is unknown.
- Sit down facing the water, keeping eyes on victim.
- Lower yourself slowly into the water to avoid unnecessary splash and/or ripples.

Beach Entry
- Run into water.
- Lift legs high to avoid tripping.
- When water deepens, lean forward and spring off one foot; do shallow dive.
- Keep body, arms, and head in streamlined position.

Shallow Dive
- Step to pool edge, feet spread slightly, toes over edge of pool deck.
- Crouch down, bend knees, hold the back parallel to water's surface.
- Lean forward, keep eyes on victim as long as possible.
- Swing arms back.
- Press against deck or pool edge with toes, extend legs.
- Swing arms forward, extended in front of head; drop head slightly; hands enter first.
- Use where water and bottom conditions are known, with a minimum depth of 5 feet.

Approach Stroking and Ready Position

Suggested Time

15 minutes

Objective   To ensure participants can demonstrate how to quickly and safely approach a victim in the water

Activity   Discuss the need for speed in making a rescue and the need to make occasional visual contact with victim. Remind participants that they must conserve enough energy to make the return trip.

Explain, demonstrate, and practice the following approach strokes and the ready position:

Approach Strokes

- Crawl stroke—As an approach stroke, keep face in water, lift head occasionally to breathe and refocus on victim.
- Breaststroke—Combines speed and energy conservation with opportunity for a quick look at victim. Allows rescuer to swim on surface or underwater and is useful in rough water.

Ready Position

- Stop forward momentum about 6 feet from victim to get into ready position.
- Assess situation; determine best rescue technique.
- Tuck legs under body and sweep arms forward, leaning on side and away from victim.
- Use sculling motion to move forward toward victim for contact.

Rescue Kicks

Suggested Time   20 minutes

Objective   To ensure that participants can demonstrate how to kick efficiently to carry a victim through the water

Activity   Explain, demonstrate, and practice the following rescue kicks:

Inverted Scissors Kick
- Like normal scissors kick, except that leg nearer surface extends back, leg farther from surface extends forward

Elementary Backstroke Kick
- Use if stronger for lifeguard than scissors kick

Rotary Kick
- Alternating breaststroke movement where each leg kicks through breaststroke range of motion
- Useful in ready position and in carrying or towing a victim

Surface Diving and Underwater Swimming

Suggested Time

25 minutes

Objective

To ensure that participants can demonstrate three ways to submerge below the surface and swim underwater

Activity

Explain, demonstrate, and practice the following:

Feetfirst Surface Dive (use in murky water or in water of unknown depth)
- Tread water.
- Press down with hands and give strong breaststroke or scissors kick. Conclusion of thrust raises body high in the water.
- Allow body to sink, hands by sides, until head is submerged and momentum slows.
- Rotate wrists, turn palms outward, press upwards with hands.
- Recover arms to the side and pull again, or level out and swim forward.

Pike or Tuck Surface Dive
- In clear water, swim breaststroke on surface until ready to dive.
- Lower head, flex at hips while pressing arms and palms backward to thighs.

- Lift and extend legs while recovering, arms forward.
- Open eyes and look down while lifting legs.
- Legs should rise above surface. Legs will be bent at the knees for tuck and straight at the knees for pike.

Quick Surface Dive
- Use crawl stroke to gain forward momentum.
- Take a breath.
- Plunge lead arm downward and bring other arm down to meet it while flexing at hips.
- Lift the legs high in air.
- Open eyes and look down while lifting legs.

Recovery of Submerged Victim by Surface Diving

Suggested Time

10 minutes

Objective

To ensure that the participant is able to help a victim who has slipped beneath the surface of the water

Activity

Refer participants to Chapter 3, pages 34 and 35 in the *Supplement.*

Explain, demonstrate, and practice the following techniques:
- If victim goes under as you are approaching, keep eyes on spot where victim disappears and and when you reach it, perform surface dive.
- Grab victim's wrist, arm, or armpit from behind.
- If bottom is firm, plant feet, push off, kick or stroke to the surface.
- If bottom is muddy or soft, depend on stroke and/or kick.

- If in doubt about victim's location, approach the surface location where victim was last seen. Look for bubbles.
- If water is clear, scan the bottom by systematically swimming across area with face in water.
- Look for light or dark areas in contrast to bottom.
- If water is murky, search using a series of systematic feetfirst dives.
- Swim along bottom for two or three body lengths, then surface.
- Move back about three feet and repeat.
- When you recover victim, begin rescue breathing as soon as possible.

Conditioning Swim

Suggested Time

10 minutes

Objective

To develop participants' strength and endurance in swimming and lifeguarding skills

Activity

Have participants swim continuously for 10 minutes using a combination of strokes such as the crawl stroke, breaststroke, and sidestroke.

Encourage participants to swim a minimum distance of 500 yards. Participants who complete this distance in the allotted time should try to increase the distance with each conditioning swim. Participants who do not complete the distance in the allotted time should keep track of the distance they did complete and attempt to increase the distance each time they swim or swim the distance in less time.

Review and Assignment

Suggested Time   5 minutes

Objective   To ensure participants' understanding of the information covered thus far in the course

Activity   Review the key points of the session. Answer any questions that participants may have. Give the following reading assignment.
- Textbook: Chapter 5, pages 5-10 through 5-13
- *Supplement:* Chapter 3, pages 35 through 43.

Session 3

Time	Approximately 2 hours, 45 minutes
Topics	Communication Systems; Surface Approaches; Swimming Assists, Tows, and Carries
References	Textbook: Chapter 5, pages 5-10 through 5-13; *Supplement*: Chapter 3, pages 35 through 43
Materials and Equipment	Chalkboard and chalk, or flip chart and markers; whistles; signal flags; rescue tube; appropriate audiovisual equipment (optional)
Facilities	Classroom and a pool or lake
Suggested Audiovisual	*Emergency Aquatic Skills:* video; Unit 5— *Approaches,* 4 minutes; Unit 6—*Swimming Assists and Tows,* 8 minutes

Note: Instructor may also choose to show the section of Unit 9—*Advanced Rescue Skills* that shows the cross-chest carries.

Review

Suggested Time	5 minutes
Objective	To verify participants' understanding of the information from the previous session
Activity	Review the key subjects and objectives of the previous session. Allow participants to bring up topics for discussion that relate to the course content.

Communication Systems

Suggested Time   15 minutes

Objective   To enable participants to use communication systems requiring whistles, hand signals, equipment signals, and flag signals

Activity   Discuss, demonstrate, and practice the use of whistles, hands, equipment, and flags as methods of communication.

Have participants form small groups and test each other on the various signals described in their reading assignment and on the circumstances or situations for which each type of communication would be most useful and appropriate.

Refer participants to pages 5-10 through 5-13 in the textbook.

Suggested Audiovisual   *Emergency Aquatic Skills:* Unit 5— *Approaches,* 4 minutes; Unit 6—*Swimming Assists and Tows,* 8 minutes

Note: The section in Unit 9 on cross-chest carries may also be shown at this time.

Break

Suggested Time   10 minutes

Activity   Participants should change clothes and prepare for the in-water skills practice.

Skills Practice: Surface Approaches, Swimming Assists, Tows and Carries

Suggested Time

Surface Approaches

45 minutes

Objective

To ensure that participants can demonstrate how to make contact with an active or passive drowning victim safely and to position that victim for an effective tow or carry

Activity

Refer participants to the *Supplement:* Chapter 3, pages 35 through 43. You may wish to demonstrate and practice tows, carries, and assists before approaches, or teach the skills together. Explain, demonstrate, and practice the following skills:

Swim or Dive to the Rear
- Used for active victim.
- Swim to a position immediately behind victim. Assume a ready position.
- Scull closer and grasp victim at the armpit to level victim to a horizontal or nearly horizontal position in the water.
- Apply a cross-chest carry.
- If return distance is greater than 40 feet, use rescue equipment or a single or double armpit tow.

Front Surface Approach
- Use if victim is facedown at or near the surface.
- Enter and swim to within 6 feet of victim.
- Stop and assume ready position.
- In ready position, scull to victim and grasp underside of victim's wrist (right hand to right wrist, or left hand to left wrist).
- Kick for momentum and pull victim's arm toward you while rotating the wrist palm up to turn victim on back.

- Use a wrist tow or any other appropriate tow to tow victim to safety, or use the cross-chest carry.

Rear Approach
- Use when victim is active or passive, on or near the surface.
- Enter water and approach to within 6 feet of victim.
- If victim is passive or the return distance is over 40 feet, use a single or double armpit tow or rescue equipment.
- If victim is active and return distance is less than 40 feet, approach, assume ready position, scull closer, and grasp victim's armpit. You may choose to use a single armpit tow (use sidestroke or elementary backstroke kick) or a cross-chest carry.

Swimming Assists

Suggested Time

10 minutes

Objective

To ensure that participants can demonstrate how to assist a victim to safety by supporting and pulling or pushing him or her

Activity

Explain, demonstrate, and practice the following:

Assist on Front or Back
- Swim alongside victim and grasp victim by upper arm near armpit (thumb up).
- Support victim and keep his or her head above water.
- Talk reassuringly and swim next to victim, using modified sidestroke or breaststroke.
- Maintain firm grip on victim.

Assist by Two Lifeguards
- Same as assist on front or back, but with one rescuer at each armpit.
- Use modified breaststroke or sidestroke.

Tows and Carries

Suggested Time

50 minutes

Objective

To ensure that participants can demonstrate how to safely and effectively support and tow or carry a distressed or drowning victim to safety

Activity

Explain, demonstrate, and practice the following:

Single Armpit Tow
- Well-suited for use with rear approach to active or passive victim.
- Assume ready position.
- Use hand that is closer to victim to grasp victim's armpit (right hand to right armpit or left hand to left).
- Place fingers under arm and into armpit with thumb up along outside of victim's arm.
- Rest your head on the water and swim elementary backstroke or sidestroke, using regular or inverted scissors kick.

Double Armpit Tow
- Use with rear approach to active or passive victim.
- Assume ready position.
- Grasp armpits simultaneously with fingers under arms and thumbs up.
- Put your head back and begin kicking until you and victim are horizontal with your legs and your lower body beneath victim.
- Keep victim's head back and arms extended.
- For more control, slide other hand under the armpits, across the chest, and hold on to wrist with opposite hand.
- If using elementary backstroke kick—
  — Assume a modified ready position by keeping body partially horizontal.
  — Do not turn on your side.

Wrist Tow

- Only for passive victim.
- Use with front surface approach.
- Turn victim on back by grabbing underside of victim's wrist (right hand to right, left hand to left).
- Lean backwards and swim while pulling victim's arm across your body, twisting wrist in line with pull.
- Swim sidestroke or elementary backstroke with towing arm fully extended along the surface of the water. Victim's arm should be extended also.

Change From Wrist Tow to Armpit Tow (Choppy Water Conditions)

- Continue to kick vigorously.
- As you pull victim forward with your hand on victim's wrist, use your free hand to grasp victim's armpit.
- Release victim's wrist and continue with single armpit tow.
- Maintain contact with victim while changing positions.

Cross-Chest Carry

- Primarily for active victim over a short distance.
- Use rear approach.
- Assume ready position 6 feet from victim.
- Make contact.
- Grasp victim's armpit.
- Kick and pull vigorously to level victim to horizontal position.
- Reach under victim's arm (right arm to right side, left to left) with free hand and cross victim's lower chest until hand is holding victim's opposite side.
- Let go of armpit and kick and stroke vigorously.

Alternate Cross-Chest Carry

- After leveling the victim to horizontal position and getting under way, bring stroking arm over corresponding shoulder of victim across chest until your hand is on victim's side just below armpit.

- Hold victim firmly and snugly against the side of your chest.
- You are on your side with your hip just beneath the small of victim's back.
- Use sidestroke with regular or inverted scissors kick.
- Check to see that victim's face is clear of the water. This carry does not allow the victim to be as clear of the water as the cross-chest carry does.

Conditioning Swim

Suggested Time   15 minutes

Objective   To develop participants' strength and endurance in swimming and lifeguarding skills

Activity   Have participants swim continuously for 15 minutes using crawl stroke, breaststroke, and sidestroke.

Review and Assignment

Suggested Time   5 minutes

Objective   To ensure participants' understanding of the material covered thus far in the course

Activity   Review the key points of this session. Answer any questions participants may have. Give the following reading assignment:
- Textbook: Chapter 5, pages 5-2 through 5-10; Chapter 8; Chapter 9, pages 9-11 through 9-13
- *Supplement:* Chapter 3, pages 43 through 47

Session 4

Time	Approximately 3 hours
Topics	Health and Sanitation; Swimming Pool Maintenance; Emergency Action Plans; Removing a Victim From the Water: Lifts, Assists, and Carries; Defense and Escapes
References	Textbook: Chapter 5, pages 5-2 through 5-10; Chapter 8; and Chapter 9, pages 9-11 through 9-13; *Supplement:* Chapter 3, pages 43 through 47.
Materials and Equipment	Chalkboard and chalk, or flip chart and markers; kit for testing chemical balance of water; appropriate audiovisual equipment (optional).
Facilities	Classroom and a pool or lake
Suggested Audiovisual	*Emergency Aquatic Skills:* Unit 8—*Defenses and Escapes,* 9 minutes; Unit 7—*Removal from the Water,* 9 minutes

Review

Suggested Time	5 minutes
Objective	To verify participants' understanding of the information from the previous session
Activity	Review the key subjects and objectives of the previous session. Allow participants to bring

up subjects for discussion that relate to the course content.

Health and Sanitation

Suggested Time 10 minutes

Objective To ensure that participants have the knowledge necessary to operate a safe, healthful, and sanitary aquatic facility

Activity Refer participants to the textbook, Chapter 8.

Briefly identify the importance of the lifeguard's involvement in the health and sanitation aspects of the daily operations of an aquatic facility. State that the amount of involvement will vary from one facility to another. Point out that this is not a course for pool operators and will only briefly cover some basics of pool operation. Encourage participants to get in-depth training in aquatic facility management or pool operation through community colleges, universities, pool chemical companies, health departments, or YMCAs.

Identify the primary factors that contribute to the safety, healthfulness, and sanitation of an aquatic facility and discuss how these factors can be influenced by the lifeguard.

These factors include—
- Personal hygiene practices of the patrons. Patrons should be required to shower before entering the pool. Patrons with open sores or skin diseases should be prohibited from using the facility.
- Safety and cleanliness of the facility. Daily inspections and maintenance should be conducted by the staff.
- Quality of the water in the swimming area. Filtration and disinfection systems should

be kept in good working order and operated only by trained personnel. At waterfront facilities, the monitoring systems established by local boards of health or other regulatory agencies must be used.
- Symptoms of overexposure to heat or cold. Lifeguards should constantly check patrons for these symptoms.

Point out that each facility should have a manual of operation that includes the following:
- A list of items to be inspected and how often each item is to be inspected
- The areas of the facility to be cleaned and the cleaning procedures to be followed
- Procedures to be followed for testing and maintaining the water quality
- Samples of all records and reports used by the lifeguard in the operation of the facility

Special Assignment—Out-of-Class

Objective
To provide participants with experience in identifying facility equipment to be inspected

Activity
Refer participants to the textbook, Chapter 8, pages 8-2 to 8-4.
Have participants identify the areas and equipment used at an aquatic facility that should be inspected on a daily basis and develop a checklist for inspecting a pool for proper health and safety conditions.

Swimming Pool Maintenance

Suggested Time
20 minutes

Objective To ensure that participants learn of the factors in pool maintenance and the responsibilities of lifeguards in regard to these factors

Activity Make arrangements for a tour of the facility and a demonstration of the systems and the water testing equipment.

Refer participants to the textbook, pages 8-4 through 8-10. Briefly discuss the following subjects:

Water Circulation—Describe components of the circulation system, such as drains, overflow troughs, gauges, skimmers, balance tank, strainers, pumps, chemical tanks.

Balanced Water—Refer participants to Fig. 8-1, page 8-5. Point out that the chemical levels discussed are not specific and may vary for different states and localities. Use a testing kit to demonstrate how to test the chemical balance of the water at your facility.

Disinfection—Refer participants to pages 8-5, 8-6, 8-9, and 8-10. Briefly identify the following disinfectants and discuss their advantages, disadvantages, and problems:

- Chlorine
- Bromine
- Iodine

Filtration—Identify the two common methods of filtration.

- Sand and gravel filters—Pump forces water through the filter. Water enters filter at top, is spread over top of sand by baffle plate, and passes through several layers of sand and gravel.
- Diatomaceous earth (DE) filters—Filter elements are coated with DE. Water passes through DE into manifold pipe and is returned to pool.

Chemical Safety—Refer participants to pages 8-9 and 8-10 in the textbook. Emphasize the importance of preventive measures to be taken with all chemicals. Point out that personnel who are handling chemicals must be properly trained in the chemical's purpose; the operation of chemical equipment; maintenance procedures; and emergency procedures related to fire, explosion, toxic gases, and facility evacuation. **Electrical Safety**—Emphasize that state electrical codes must be complied with in all aquatic facilities. Caution participants about the use of any electrical appliance around the water. Remind participants that pools should be empty of patrons when facility staff are vacuuming.

Emergency Action Plans

Suggested Time

25 minutes

Objective

To introduce participants to various emergency plans and have participants evaluate the procedures to be followed in developing such plans

Activity

Refer participants to the textbook, pages 5-2 to 5-10.

Discuss the procedures to be used in establishing emergency action plans for aquatic facilities:

- Establish a chain of command in order to designate limits and lines of authority and responsibility.
- Check state and local ordinances for information on required equipment and limits of authority.
- Review and analyze records of previous accidents and emergencies at the facility.
- Involve support personnel from police, fire, and rescue departments when developing plans.
- Identify the facility's first aid station.

- Assign primary and secondary responsibilities to all facility staff.
- Survey all equipment and then project needs.
- Set up a records and reports system.
- Designate a media liaison from the facility staff.
- Outline crowd-control procedures.

Have participants "walk through" action plans for various emergencies. Discuss the advantages and disadvantages of the plans. Relate the discussion to visibility, reaction time, backup availability, and support personnel.

Emergency Action Plans for Multistaff Facility

- Non-life-threatening emergencies
  —Minor emergency, such as a child with an abrasion
  —Major emergency, such as a broken bone
- Life-threatening emergency, such as a drowning in progress

Emergency Action Plans for Single-Lifeguard Facility

- Discuss procedures for similar situations.

Special Assignment

Suggested Time

15 minutes

Objective

To ensure that participants can formulate an emergency action plan

Activity

Divide the class into groups of three to five participants.
Part 1
Have each group draw a diagram of a facility. The diagram should show the areas and zones of scanning for each guard on duty.

Part 2

Have each group decide on an accident scenario, describe an accident, and explain what the emergency action plan would be for each staff member on duty.

The accident scenario should describe the accident, injury or injuries to the victim or victims, the location of the facility, and the number of patrons at the facility.

Avoid ideal situations. Plans should be realistic and within the limits of available resources. Groups should be prepared to present the plans during class, if time permits.

Suggested Audiovisual *Emergency Aquatic Skills:* Unit 7—*Removal from the Water;* 9 minutes

Break

Suggested Time 10 minutes

Activity Participants should change clothes and prepare for the in-water skills practice.

Skills Practice: Removing a Victim From the Water: Lifts, Assists, and Carries; Defense and Escapes; Multiple Near-Drowning Maneuver

Removing a Victim From the Water: Lifts, Assists, and Carries

Suggested Time 15 minutes

Objective	To ensure that participants can demonstrate the ability to remove victims from the water in such a way as to prevent further injury
	Note: For practice sessions, have participants pair off with someone of comparable size.
	Refer participants to the textbook, pages 9-12, 9-13, and 9-14.
Activity	Explain, demonstrate, and practice each of the following skills. Emphasize safety for both the victim and the lifeguard.

- **Lift From Water**—Protect the victim's head and body. Use legs, not the back, for power when lifting.
- **Shallow Water Assist**—Maintain a firm grip on the wrist of the victim's arm that goes across lifeguard's shoulders.
- **Beach Drag**—Use when the victim is unconscious or heavy or where there is a sloping beach. Stress the importance of the lifeguard keeping his or her back straight and protecting the victim's head.
- **Pack-Strap Carry**—Emphasize balance and slow movements. This carry must never be used if there is the slightest possibility that the victim has a neck or back injury.

Note: For both the shallow water assist and the beach drag, you can use two people if another person is available to assist you.

Defense and Escapes

Suggested Time	40 minutes
Objective	To ensure that participants will be able to identify the various options available to them

victim who attempts to grab them

Refer participants to the *Supplement,* Chapter 3, pages 43 through 47.

Suggested Audiovisual   *Emergency Aquatic Skills:* Unit 8—*Defenses and Escapes,* 9 minutes

Activity   Discuss briefly the following circumstances in which a lifeguard may be grabbed by a panicky victim:
- Improper approach by lifeguard
- Multiple victims
- Improper carry by lifeguard
- Poor visibility

Describe the typical reaction of a drowning victim who is able to grab a rescuer.
- Typically, victim grabs rescuer's head, since it is the only or largest body part out of water, but victim may also grab rescuer's wrist or arm.
- Victim wants to use rescuer in order to keep afloat and breathe.

Defense

Suggested Time   10 minutes

Objective   To ensure that participants can demonstrate the ability to use a one-hand or two-hand block to safely defend against a victim who attempts to grab them

Activity   Demonstrate and practice:
1. One-hand block
   — Place the open palm of one hand high on the victim's chest.

— Lean away and submerge when victim attempts to grab you.
2. Two-hand block
— Block with two hands high on victim's chest. Submerge.

In either block, return quickly to surface and approach victim from behind.

Escapes

Suggested Time

35 minutes

Objective

To ensure that participants can demonstrate how to rescue a victim who has grabbed them by the head or arm by swimming the victim to safety, by submerging with victim, or by using an escape

Note: Instruct participants to signal "let go" to each other by a predetermined signal, such as two taps.

Activity

Option 1: Swim to Safety With Victim Holding On
- Use with small, bouyant victim or when close to safety.
- Use breaststroke if victim grabs you from the front.
- Use sidestroke or breaststroke if victim grabs you by the head from the front or from behind.
- Use sidestroke if victim grabs you by the wrist or upper arm.

Option 2: Submerge Victim to Break Contact
- For front and rear head holds, do the following:
  — Take a breath.
  — Tuck the chin.
  — Turn your head to one side.
  — Raise your shoulders.

- Dive feet first, taking victim underwater.
- For wrist or upper arm holds, do the following:
  - Place free hand on victim's shoulder.
  - Press victim under water and pull your hand free.
- Return to surface away from victim.
- Swim to rear of victim and use an appropriate carry.

Option 3: Escape and Rescue

1. Front head-hold escape
   - When grabbed by your head from the front, take a quick breath, tuck your chin, submerge with victim.
   - Turn head to the side and raise shoulders.
   - On the way down, bring your hands to the victim's elbows, thumbs on inside, fingers on outside.
   - Push up and away from you, keeping chin tucked and shoulders raised.
   - When free, swim on back or side out of reach.
   - Approach victim from rear and use an appropriate tow or carry.

2. Rear head-hold escape
   - If victim grabs you from behind, take a quick breath, tuck chin, raise shoulders, submerge with victim.
   - Bring your hands to underside of victim's arms on or just above elbows.
   - Push upwards forcefully and twist your head and shoulders out until you escape.
   - Swim out of reach.
   - Approach victim from rear and use an appropriate tow or carry.

3. Wrist-grip escape
   - If victim grabs your arm or wrist, submerge victim by pushing on

victim's shoulder with your free hand
while kicking upward.
— Pull your hand free.
— You may also reach down with free
hand, grab your other hand, and jerk
upward quickly and firmly to free it.
— Stroke backwards quickly with arms
and legs to get out of reach.
— Use rear approach and appropriate tow
or carry.

Multiple Near-Drowning Maneuver

Suggested Time

15 minutes

Objective

To ensure that participants can demonstrate
options for rescuing multiple near-drowning
victims

Activity

Explain the following:
• A multiple near-drowning situation should
be handled by more than one lifeguard,
preferably a ratio of one lifeguard to each
victim.
• If only one lifeguard is available, and
victims are within a short distance to
safety, tow or push victims clutching each
other to safety, using double armpit tow
on one victim.
Demonstrate and practice the following:
• If victims are too deep to push or pull to
safety, do the following:
— Swim to rear of victim who is in the top
position.
— Move hands to armpits of that victim
and place your feet on other victim's
upper chest.
— Press down on chest with your feet and
pull on armpits of victim in the top
position with your hands until the two
are separated.
— Tow or carry first victim to safety.

74

— Return to other victim or use second rescuer, if one is available, to assist the other victim.

Conditioning Swim

Suggested Time   15 minutes

Objective   To develop participants' strength and endurance in swimming and lifeguarding skills

Activity   Have participants swim continuously for 15 minutes using a combination of strokes such as the crawl stroke, breaststroke, and sidestroke.

Review and Assignment

Suggested Time   5 minutes

Objective   To ensure participants' understanding of information covered to this point in the course

Activity   Review the key points of the session. Answer any questions that participants may have at this time. Give the following reading assignment:
• Textbook: Chapter 7, pages 7-3 through 7-7; Chapter 9, pages 9-20 through 9-23
• *Supplement*: Chapter 1, pages 10 through 15 and Chapter 5.

Session 5

Time	Approximately 3 hours
Topics	Special Situations; Rescue Equipment; Using Rescue Equipment
References	Textbook: Chapter 7, pages 7-3 through 7-7; Chapter 9, pages 9-20 through 9-23; *Supplement:* Chapter 1, pages 10 through 15; and Chapter 5
Materials and Equipment	Chalkboard and chalk, or flip chart and markers, rescue tube, rescue board or surfboard; appropriate audiovisual equipment (optional)
Facilities	Classroom and a pool or lake
Suggested Audiovisual	*Emergency Aquatic Skills:* Unit 9—*Advanced Rescue Skills,* 15 minutes

Review

Suggested Time	5 minutes
Objective	To verify participants' understanding of the information covered in the previous session
Activity	Review the key subjects and objectives of the preceding session.

Special Situations

Suggested Time   40 minutes

Hypothermia and Exposure to Cold Temperatures

Objective   To enable participants to recognize and treat victims suffering from hypothermia and exposure to cold temperatures

Activity   Refer participants to Chapter 5 in the *Supplement.* Briefly discuss the factors that influence the onset of hypothermia, including—
- Air and water temperatures.
- Wind speed.
- Length of exposure.
- Amount and type of clothing worn.
- The individual's age, size, and body build.
- The mental and physical condition of the individual.

Emphasize the four processes through which the body loses heat.
- Conduction—Heat lost through body contact with a cold object, such as water or the ground.
- Convection—Heat lost through air or water movement around the body.
- Radiation—Heat lost to still air that surrounds the body, such as cold air with no wind.
- Evaporation—Heat lost through water evaporating on the skin, such as perspiration.

Discuss body reactions to decreases in body-core temperature. Refer participants to Chapter 5, pages 72 through 75 in the *Supplement.*

Discuss the first aid steps for victims who are in the following categories:

Mild to Moderate Hypothermia

- Move the victim to a warm indoor area.
- Cover the victim with a blanket until symptoms disappear.
- Give warm, noncaffeinated liquids.
- Do not give the victim alcohol.

Severe to Critical Hypothermia

- Keep victim in horizontal position, and call EMS immediately.
- Do not allow the victim to move around and do not rub or massage the victim's extremities. Any form of exercise increases the flow of cold blood from the extremities back into the body core, increasing the chances for "afterdrop."
- Prevent heat loss by removing wet clothing.
- Wrap the victim in blankets, dry towels, several layers of clothing, or all of these items. Do not use hot objects or high temperatures. Use hot water bottles, heating pads, or chemical heat packs if available. Wrap these items in towels or blankets to keep the victim from being burned. Use them to rewarm trunk, groin, neck, and head only.
- Provide warm, dry clothing. Allow the body temperature to return to normal gradually.
- Do not heat the extremities.
- Maintain an open airway and perform rescue breathing (mouth-to-mouth resuscitation) or CPR if necessary. (Before starting CPR, you may need to check

victim's pulse for up to 1 minute because of slower pulse rate in hypothermia.)
- Give warm liquids if the victim is conscious and able to swallow.
- Do not give the victim any alcohol or beverages containing caffeine.
- Do not allow the victim to smoke.
- Be sure the victim receives immediate medical care.

Refer participants to pages 9-20 to 9-23 in the textbook.

Identify the following body reactions to sudden immersion in cold water and their consequences:
- A gasp reflex, often a sudden uncontrollable attempt to "catch one's breath," can cause a person whose face is submerged to breathe water in.
- Hyperventilation, the rapid breathing in of oxygen and blowing off of carbon dioxide, can also result in a person whose face is submerged breathing water in.
- An increase in the heart rate and a change in the blood pressure can cause cardiac arrest or abnormal and irregular heartbeat rhythm.

Discuss the following preventive measures that individuals may take:
- Dress properly, with layers of lightweight clothing.
- Always wear a personal floatation device (PFD) when boating on cold water.
- Never go boating alone.

Discuss the following self-help behavior that individuals should use if they cannot get out of the water immediately.
- Put on a PFD as soon as possible.
- Check to see that everyone is all right.

Have participants give you the reasons for the three procedures individuals **do not** follow.

- **Do not** attempt to swim to shore. (Physical activity releases heat and permits cold water to flow through clothing, thus chilling the body more rapidly.)
- **Do not** remove any clothing. (Clothing provides some insulation against heat loss.)
- **Do not** perform survival floating. (This necessitates putting the face in the water, which causes heat loss.)

Emphasize that protection is critical. Demonstrate and discuss the HELP and HUDDLE positions.

- HELP position. Point out the importance of achieving a good balance position by lowering the thighs, if necessary. Refer participants to textbook, Fig. 9-15, page 9-21.
- HUDDLE position. Stress victims keeping the sides of their chests touching. Refer participants to the textbook, Fig. 9-16, page 9-21.

Describe body reactions during the mammalian diving reflex.

- Blood flow is reduced to most parts of the body except the heart, lungs, and brain.
- Oxygen-carrying blood conserves heat and maintains normal functioning of the vital organs.

Discuss rescues in cold water. Ask participants to cite some factors that increase victim's survival chances.

- Immersion of the face. Mammalian diving reflex may occur in water 70°F or colder.

- Victim's age. Mammalian diving reflex is believed to occur more often in younger victims.
- Water temperature. Colder water may cause a stronger mammalian diving reflex.
- Laryngospasm. Water may go to stomach, not lungs, because spasm of larynx may close airway.

Ask participants to cite the procedures for dealing with a submerged cold water victim who has been removed from the water.
- Start rescue breathing.
- Begin first aid for hypothermia.
- Get medical care for victim as soon as possible.

Ask participants to describe the vital signs that indicate the core temperature is approaching normal.
- Return of normal skin color
- Contracting of pupils
- Increase in rate and depth of breathing
- Increase in pulse rate and strength

Point out that in-service training programs should concentrate on—
- Procedures for cold water rescues.
- Lifeguard cautions, such as not attempting these rescues without assistance.
- Use of rescue boats.
- The dangers of thermoclines (a sharp change of temperature from one layer of water to another).

Heat Emergencies

Objective To enable participants to identify and treat victims of heat exhaustion, heat stroke, and heat cramps

Activity   Refer participants to Chapter 5 in the
Supplement, pages 75 and 76. Briefly discuss
the need for protection against the sun and
methods to achieve it.
     Write "Heat Stroke" and "Heat Exhaustion"
as headings for two columns on the
chalkboard or flip chart. Have participants tell
you the signs and symptoms of each and how
to care for each.

Heat Stroke   Heat Exhaustion

Signs and Symptoms

Heat Stroke	Heat Exhaustion
• Hot, red skin	• Cool, pale, moist skin
• Very high temperature	• Rapid, weak pulse
• Shock or unconsciousness	• Weakness/dizziness
	• Nausea/vomiting

What to Do

Heat Stroke	Heat Exhaustion
• Call EMS.	• Call EMS.
• Get victim into coolest place available.	• Get victim into coolest place available.
• Cool by immersing in cool bath or wrapping in wet sheets and fanning.	• Place victim on back with feet elevated.
• Care for shock by placing victim lying down on back with feet elevated	• Cool by applying wet sheets and by fanning.
	• Give $1/2$ glass of water every 15 minutes if victim is conscious and can tolerate it.

Make another column headed "Heat Cramps."
Have the participants give you the information
for each category.

Heat Cramps

Signs and Symptoms

- Muscular spasms and pains, usually in the legs or abdomen.

What to Do

- Get victim into coolest place available.

- Give $^1/_2$ glass of water every 15 minutes for an hour.

Prevention

- Seek protection from sun and extreme heat.

- Replace fluids by drinking water, sports drinks, or fruit juices.

Seizures

Objective   To ensure participants will recognize the symptoms of a seizure and know the procedures to follow when rescuing a seizure victim

Activity   Refer participants to Chapter 5, pages 76 through 78 in the *Supplement*. Explain and discuss the procedures for rescuing and caring for the victim of a seizure while in the water. Emphasize the following points:
- Victim will go underwater quickly without warning.
- Victim will not be able to assist in own rescue.

- Victim will not be able to assist in own rescue.
- Support victim in the water, keeping head and face above the water, head tilted back to keep airway open.
- Keep a victim having muscular contractions away from sides of pool or dock to avoid injury.
- Victim can breathe in large amounts of water.
- Remove victim from the water as soon as possible.
- Check victim's breathing and pulse after removal from the water. Victim may need rescue breathing.
- Place victim on side to allow fluids to drain from the mouth.
- EMS should be called.

Have participants describe the signs and symptoms of a grand mal seizure.
- An aura. Victim may have hallucinations, a painful sensation, a peculiar taste in mouth, an awareness of a smell, or a sensation warning victim to move to safety.
- Rigidity of the body, which may be preceded by a high-pitched cry.
- Loss of consciousness.
- Uncoordinated muscle movements. Victim may lose bladder and bowel control, salivate, hold the breath. Heart rate will increase.
- Drooling and frothing at the mouth may occur.
- Drowsiness and confusion may occur afterwards. Victim will gradually regain consciousness and complain of a headache.

Briefly discuss first aid procedures for seizure victims. Have participants give you the seven points listed on page 77 in the

Supplement and list them on the chalkboard or flip chart.

- Prevent victim from being injured. Clear area of hard or sharp objects, loosen tight clothing.
- Do not restrain victim if he or she is having muscular contractions.
- Do not place anything in victim's mouth.
- Turn victim on side, if necessary, for fluid to drain from mouth.
- Have someone call EMS.
- Stay with victim until EMS arrives. Monitor breathing and begin rescue breathing if breathing stops.
- Provide victim with a place to rest, privacy, and reassurance.

Rescue Equipment

Suggested Time   5 minutes

Objective   To ensure that participants can describe various kinds of rescue equipment

Activity   Refer participants to the textbook, pages 7-4 through 7-7, and 9-11 through 9-13. Briefly discuss the following pieces of rescue equipment that may be found at an aquatic facility:

- **Rescue Tube**—Made of soft, strong foam material. Strap molded into the tube with a ring on one end and a snap hook at the other. Shoulder strap and a 6-foot line are attached to the ring end of the tube.
- **Rescue Buoy**—Made of lightweight, hard, buoyant plastic. Handgrips are molded on each side. Line with a shoulder strap is attached to one end of the buoy.
- **Torpedo Buoy**—Generally made of plastic with handholds or grip ropes on

sides. Smaller versions have tow rope and shoulder strap. Larger versions usually attached to a line that is fed out from shore.

- **Lines and Reels**—Have approximately 500 to 600 feet of line on a reel. Eye splice or a snap hook on the free end of the line allows the lifeguard to make a shoulder loop or to attach line to rescue tube or rescue buoy. Second lifeguard is needed to to keep the reel from fouling or snagging and to reel in the line.
- **Backboard**—Made of aluminum or wood.
- **Litters and Stretchers**—Used for emergency transportation. They have aluminum or wooden handles and a canvas or vinyl bed.
- **Rescue Board**—Is larger and has more flotation than a surfboard. It can readily support a victim and a lifeguard.
- **Rescue Boat**—Can be a rowboat, canoe, or powerboat. The lifeguard has two options when using the boat to make contact with a victim: (1) extending an object to the victim or (2) entering the water to make a rescue, if a second lifeguard is in the boat.
- **Swim Fins**—Allow a lifeguard to cover a distance in less time. Fins are helpful in diving to the bottom of a deep pool. They can be used to stabilize both the victim and the lifeguard if the lifeguard must administer rescue breathing (mouth-to-mouth resuscitation) in deep water or suspects spinal injury.

Suggested Audiovisual

Emergency Aquatic Skills: Unit 9—*Advanced Rescue Skills*, 15 minutes

Note: At this time, you may wish to show only

that portion of Unit 9 that shows the use of the rescue board.

Break

Suggested Time   10 minutes

Activity   Participants should change clothes and prepare for the in-water skills practice.

Skills Practice: Using Rescue Equipment

Suggested Time

Using Rescue Equipment

1 hour, 20 minutes

Objective   To ensure that participants can demonstrate the use of a rescue tube or buoy and a rescue board to rescue a victim

Activity   Discuss the following advantages of using rescue equipment.
- Safety—Lifeguard keeps the equipment between himself or herself and the victim.
- Freedom—Lifeguard has better use of hands and legs to move in the water.
- Flotation—Lifeguard uses the flotation of the equipment to its best advantage when supporting himself or herself or the victim.
- Energy—Proper use of the equipment conserves the lifeguard's energy.

Refer participants to the *Supplement*: Chapter 1, pages 10 through 15.

Rescue Board (Active Victim)
Demonstrate and practice:

1. Launching the board
   - Place in water about knee level.
   - Hold onto sides midway and push board in front of you.
   - While moving forward, get onto the board, knees shoulder-width apart, paddle in kneeling position or lie on your stomach.
   - To launch board more quickly, hold board flat and vertically in front of you, run into water, drop board forward and flat on water. Get on in kneeling position, knees shoulder-width apart, or lie down, and paddle.
2. Approaching the victim
   - In quiet water, use crawl or butterfly arm stroke, with head up and eyes on victim.
   - In large waves about to break, flatten out on board, head down, and hold onto sides of board.
3. Rescue of tired victim able to get on the board
   - Paddle in prone position and approach victim from the side.
   - Grasp victim's nearer hand or wrist and slide off board on side opposite victim.
   - Help victim extend arms across board and rest.
   - Turn board toward shore and hold board steady so victim can swim aboard facing forward and lie on his or her stomach on board.
   - Get on board and lie down between victim's legs.
   - Adjust position so that front of board clears the water and paddle to shore.
4. Rescuing panicky or tired victim unable to get on the board
   - Approach from the side.

- Grab victim's wrist and slide off board on opposite side of victim, flipping the board over at the same time.
- Hold victim's wrists across edge of board.
- Explain what you are going to do next.
- Turn board and point toward shore.
- Place victim's arms across the board, reach across board, and roll board toward you to right it, rolling victim's chest across and onto board.
- Rotate victim so victim is lying on middle of board, head toward front.
- Swim onto board behind victim and start to paddle in lying down position toward shore.

Rescue Tube and Rescue Buoy

Demonstrate and practice:
1. Use of the tube in a throwing assist
   - Clip ends of tube together.
   - Throw tube with one hand, hold onto webbing loop with the other.
   - When victim grasps tube, pull victim to safety.
2. Rescue with rescue tube or rescue buoy
   - Hold tube or buoy in one hand, loop strap over one shoulder and under opposite arm.
   - Use stride-jump entry from elevation 3 feet high or less.
   - Let tube or buoy free in midair and when you hit the water, start stroking. If entering from higher than 3 feet, hold tube or buoy across your chest with your armpits hooked over ends.
   - At a beach, run into water, make shallow dive forward while letting go of tube or buoy but keeping strap over shoulder.
   - If entering from rocks where you know the water depth but you can't wade in,

loop strap over one shoulder and hold tube lengthwise against chest and stomach while doing a flat shallow dive. Do not use buoy for this entry.

- When within 5 or 6 feet of victim, assume ready position.
- Extend tube or buoy to victim. (If victim is panicky or excited, slip out of shoulder loop to avoid being pulled closer.)
- Calm victim and tow by holding onto the strap.

3. Rescue tube clasped around victim
   - Approach victim from the rear. Assume a ready position. Level victim.
   - Wrap tube around victim and clip ends together.
   - Position victim on back and tow.

4. Rescue tube clasped around lifeguard
   - Clip tube around your upper body.
   - Approach and contact victim.
   - Carry or tow victim using cross-chest carry or armpit tow.

5. Rescue tube with trail line attached
   - Victim grabs tube and slides head and chest about halfway up tube, holding onto sides.
   - Straddle victim from rear with your arms, reaching under victim's arms to hold sides of tube.
   - Rescuers on shore haul you and victim to safety.

Conditioning Swim

Suggested Time   25 minutes

Objective   To develop participants' strength, endurance, and technique in swimming and lifeguarding skills

Activity   Have participants review and practice
approaches, carries, tows, defense, and
escapes

Review and Assignment

**Suggested
Time**   5 minutes

Objective   To ensure that participants understand the
information covered thus far in the course

Activity   Review the key points of the session. Answer
any questions participants might have. Give
the following reading assignments:
•   Textbook: Chapter 6; Chapter 7, pages 7-1
through 7-3; Chapter 9, pages 9-4 through 9-11;
and Appendix B
•   *Supplement*: Chapter 3, pages 47 and 48

Session 6

Time	Approximately 3 hours
Topics	Records and Reports; Personal and Safety Equipment; Rescue Breathing; Rescue Equipment and Rescue Breathing
References	Textbook: Chapter 6; Chapter 7, pages 7-1 through 7-13; Chapter 9, pages 9-4 through 9-11; and Appendix B; *Supplement:* Chapter 3, pages 47 and 48
Materials and Equipment	Chalkboard and chalk, or flip chart and markers; samples of records and reports; rescue tubes, rescue buoys, and rescue boards; appropriate audiovisual equipment (optional)
Facilities	Classroom and a pool or lake
Suggested Audiovisual	*Emergency Aquatic Skills:* Unit 9—*Advanced Rescue Skills,* 15 minutes

Review

Suggested Time	5 minutes
Objective	To verify participants' understanding of the information covered in the previous session and answer any questions participants may have
Activity	Review briefly the key subjects and objectives of the previous session.

Records and Reports

Suggested Time

30 minutes

Objective

To ensure that participants are familiar with the various types of records and reports used at aquatic facilities and are aware of the necessity for records and reports systems

Activity

Refer participants to the textbook, pages 6-1 and 6-2.

Briefly discuss the following reasons for keeping accurate records and reports:

- To provide data to make decisions regarding equipment, schedules, personnel, procedures, and improvements
- To provide data concerning injuries or fatalities
- To provide a basis for budget recommendations and expenditures
- To comply with state and local ordinances regarding sanitation and maintenance
- To provide documentation of accidents and incidents for use in possible legal action

Explain the various types of records and their uses. Refer participants to the textbook, pages 6-2 to 6-8, and to Appendix B.

Write "Emergency Telephone Numbers" on the chalkboard or flip chart and have participants give you a list of the emergency telephone numbers that all facilities should have posted and any additional numbers that might be needed.

Have participants tell you the specific information that should be given to emergency personnel.

If class time permits, have participants fill in one of the sample accident reports in

Appendix B with information using an imagined accident scenario or one that the participant has witnessed, or have participants do the exercise outside of class as a special assignment.

Personal and Safety Equipment

Suggested Time   10 minutes

Objective   To familiarize participants with various items of personal and safety equipment and with their use and care

Activity   Refer participants to the textbook, pages 7-1 through 7-3.
Discuss briefly the items that may be part of the uniform requirements for lifeguards.
- Swimsuit
- Shirt
- Jacket
- Hat
- Foul-weather gear
- Whistle
- Sunglasses
- Shoes

Additional equipment may include the following:
- Binoculars
- Blankets
- Suntan lotion or sunblock

Emphasize the need for the proper care of this equipment.

Discuss the following safety equipment:
- Lifelines
- Lifeguard stands

Break

**Suggested
Time**   10 minutes

Activity   Participants should change clothes and
prepare for the in-water skills practice.

Skills Practice: Rescue Breathing; Rescue Equipment and Rescue Breathing

                Rescue Breathing

**Suggested
Time**   30 minutes

Objective   To enable participants to administer rescue
breathing in both deep water and shallow
water

Note: Some participants may not yet have
learned rescue breathing and CPR techniques.
By the end of the Lifeguard Training course, all
participants should have learned to perform
rescue breathing and CPR by taking the
American Red Cross Standard First Aid course
or equivalent courses. If participants have not
learned rescue breathing technique by this
point in the Lifeguard Training course, take
additional time to demonstrate the technique
and have participants practice it.

Refer to the *Rescue Breathing and Choking
Supplement* (Stock No. 329286). On the deck,
divide participants into groups of two.
Demonstrate and practice to achieve
proficiency in rescue breathing, including
proper victim placement and position, hand
position on victim's forehead, open position
for the airway, and pulse check. Simulate
actual rescue breaths.

Activity   Refer participants to the *Supplement:* Chapter 3, pages 47 and 48. Discuss, demonstrate, and practice the following:

Shallow Water Rescue Breathing
- In shallow water, position victim on the back so that his or her head is positioned near your left arm.
- Call for help.
- Reach your right hand between victim's right arm and side.
- Slide your hand palm up under victim's back to provide support.
- Place your left hand on victim's forehead.
- Open the airway and check for breathing.
- If victim is not breathing, pinch nose and give two full breaths.
- Check for pulse.
- If victim has pulse but is not breathing, continue rescue breathing.
- If victim has no pulse, remove victim from the water as soon as possible and begin CPR.

Deep Water Rescue Breathing
- If victim cannot be brought to shallow water or removed from pool, take victim to pool's edge.
- Grab the poolside with free hand.
- Call for help.
- Pull victim in close to the side of the pool between you and the wall.
- Position victim lying horizontal on the water parallel to the wall.
- Place both of your feet on the wall and support victim on your knees.
- Reach between victim's right arm and side with your right arm or between victim's left arm and side with your left arm.
- Slide your free arm under victim's back and grasp the pool side.
- Place your other hand on victim's forehead.

- Open the airway and check for breathing. If victim is not breathing, pinch the nose with your index finger and thumb and give two full breaths. Check for pulse. If there is a pulse but no breathing, continue rescue breathing.
- If victim has no pulse, remove victim from the water as soon as possible and begin CPR.

Rescue Equipment and Rescue Breathing

Suggested Time

1 hour

Objective

To ensure that participants can demonstrate the use of the rescue tube, rescue buoy, and rescue board to rescue a passive or unconscious victim and to support the victim while performing rescue breathing (mouth-to-mouth resuscitation)

Activity

Discuss, demonstrate, and practice using rescue equipment to rescue a passive or unconscious victim and to support that victim while administering rescue breathing (mouth-to-mouth resuscitation) in the water. Emphasize the following points:
- Stability—The lifeguard is not floundering around in the water with the victim.
- Positioning of equipment—The lifeguard positions equipment on himself or herself or on the victim to get the greatest flotation effect.
- Proper hand positioning—The lifeguard properly positions his or her hand to control the victim's body movement (do-si-do position) and to maintain an open airway. (To get into the do-si-do position, the lifeguard uses the hand closer to the victim's feet to reach over the victim's inside arm under the back, over the other

arm, and grasp the side of the pool or a rescue tube.)
- Proper body positioning—The lifeguard is able to assume a proper position to administer rescue breathing (mouth-to-mouth resuscitation).

Rescue Tube
Use the material and illustrations in the textbook on pages 9-4 to 9-8 to lead participants through the following approaches using the rescue tube:
- Front-surface approach
- Front-surface approach—alternate method
- Rear approach
- Straddle the tube

Note: For references in the textbook to certain approaches as described in the Advanced Lifesaving course, refer participants to these approaches as described in the *Lifeguard Training Supplement.*

Rescue Buoy
Use the material and illustrations in the textbook on pages 9-8 through 9-10 to guide participants through the following approaches using the rescue buoy:
- Front-surface approach—buoy to victim's back
- Front-surface approach—buoy to victim's side
- Rear approach

Rescue Board
Use the directions and illustrations in the textbook on pages 9-10 and 9-11 to guide participants through using a rescue board to assist in giving rescue breathing to a nonbreathing victim.

Conditioning Swim

Suggested Time   20 minutes

Objective   To develop participants' strength, endurance, and techniques in swimming and lifeguarding skills

Activity   Have participants pair off. Practice swimming rescues with sprint approaches of 25 yards. Use tows, carries, and escapes. Practice:
A. Front-surface approach, wrist tow
B. Rear approach, cross-chest carry
C. Swim or dive to the rear, armpit tow
D. Front, rear, and wrist-grip escapes

Review and Assignment

Suggested Time   5 minutes

Objective   To ensure participants' understanding of information covered thus far in the course

Activity   Review the key points of the session. Answer any questions that participants may have at this time. Give participants the following reading assignment:
- *Supplement:* Chapter 4

Session 7

Time	Approximately 2 hours, 40 minutes
Topics	Spinal Injuries
References	*Supplement:* Chapter 4
Materials and Equipment	Chalkboard and chalk, or flip chart and markers; backboards, ties or straps, cervical collars; appropriate audiovisual equipment (optional)
Facilities	Classroom and a pool or lake
Suggested Audiovisual	*Spinal Injury Management,* 25 minutes
	Note: Showing the audiovisual *Spinal Injury Management* is at the option of the instructor but is strongly recommended to aid in clarifying the maneuvers and techniques in managing injuries of this sort.

Review

Suggested Time	5 minutes
Objective	To verify participants' understanding of the information from the previous session
Activity	Review the key subjects and objectives of the previous session. Allow participants to bring up subjects for discussion that relate to the course content.

Spinal Injuries

Suggested Time
30 minutes

Objective
To instruct participants on procedures and techniques for handling suspected spinal injuries in the water

Suggested Audiovisual
Spinal Injury Management,
25 minutes (strongly recommended)

Note: The instructor may prefer to show this audiovisual just before the break or just before beginning skills practice.

Activity
Refer participants to the *Supplement*, Chapter 4. Have participants refer to the illustrations in the chapter as you discuss the techniques.
Briefly discuss the following points:

Anatomy and Function of the Spine
- The spine is a strong, flexible column that supports the head and the trunk and encloses and provides protection to the spinal cord.
- Vertebrae are small circles of bone that form the spinal column.
- Cushions of cartilage called intervertebral disks separate the vertebrae and allow the back to twist and bend.
- The spinal cord runs through the hollow part of the vertebrae.
- Nerve branches extend to various parts of the body through openings on the sides of the vertebrae.
- The five regions of the spine are the cervical or neck region, the thoracic or midback region, the lumbar or lower back region, the sacrum, and the coccyx.

- Injuries to the spinal column can sever or compress the spinal cord, which can result in paralysis or death.

Situations That May Indicate Spinal Injury
- Any fall from a height greater than the victim's height
- Any person found unconscious or submerged in shallow water for an unknown reason
- Any significant head trauma
- All diving accidents

Signs and Symptoms of a Possible Spinal Injury
- Pain at the site of the fracture
- Loss of movement in the extremities or below the fracture site
- Loss of sensation or tingling in the extremities
- Disorientation
- Back or neck deformity
- Visible bruising over an area of the spinal column
- Impaired breathing
- Head injury
- Fluid/blood in ears

Explain and discuss the general procedures for handling a suspected spinal injury in the water. Point out the following factors that influence the lifeguard's actions:
- Victim's condition (presence or absence of breathing or pulse)
- Lifeguard's size (compared to the victim)
- Location of the victim (shallow water, deep water, on the bottom)
- Availability of assistance (additional lifeguards, EMS, police or fire department personnel, or bystanders)
- Temperature of water and/or air

Discuss the importance of proper management of the victim's airway at all times. Explain that the victim may not be breathing or may be having difficulty breathing. Chest muscles may be paralyzed. If the victim can speak, then he or she is breathing. Otherwise, the rescuer must follow the "look, listen, and feel for breathing" steps and must start rescue breathing at once, if necessary. Care must be taken not to move the head, so the modified jaw thrust should be used to open the airway.

Explain that in the water the modified jaw thrust is best performed with a second rescuer who performs the technique while the first rescuer stabilizes the head. From a position at an angle behind the victim's head, the second rescuer places his or her hands on both sides of the victim's head and applies pressure to the angles of the lower jaw with the fingers to lift the jaw upward. At the same time, the palms of the rescuer's hands keep the victim's head from moving backwards. Detailed steps for learning the modified jaw thrust are given in the American Red Cross CPR: Basic Life Support for the Professional Rescuer course.

Emphasize the following general rescue procedures:

- Activate facility's emergency action plan.
- Approach victim carefully and minimize water movement. No jumping or diving into a position near victim.
- Reduce or prevent any movement of victim's spine. Victim's head, neck, and back must be immobilized.
- Move victim to the surface of the water, if necessary.
- Rotate victim, if necessary, to a horizontal position. Victim's face must be kept out of the water.

- Move victim to shallow water, if possible, to allow for ease of care.
- Swim fins are helpful in keeping a victim afloat in deep water.
- Check for breathing. Use a second rescuer to open the victim's airway, using the modified jaw thrust. If the victim is not breathing, start rescue breathing as soon as possible. If victim is breathing, second rescuer must monitor victim's breathing.
- Position the backboard under victim, avoiding any unnecessary movement of victim.
- Secure victim to the backboard. Strapping prevents additional injury to the spine. Use a rigid cervical collar, a blanket or towel roll, and multiple straps or cravats.
- Remove victim from the water.
- Once on deck, give first aid for shock.
- Monitor breathing and circulation until EMS personnel arrive.
- Keep the victim warm. Hypothermia is a serious threat.

Point out that participants will see these techniques demonstrated and then will practice them in the water.

Point out the following considerations when choosing a rescue technique:
- Buoyancy of victim
- Buoyancy of lifeguard
- Victim's size
- Lifeguard's size and leg-stroke power
- Lifeguard's breath-holding capacity
- Position of victim—facedown or faceup
- Location of victim—deep or shallow water, on or near the surface or underwater
- Wind and water conditions

Break

Suggested Time 10 minutes

Activity Participants should change clothes and prepare for the in-water skills practice.

Skills Practice: Spinal Injuries—Shallow Water, Deep Water

Objective

Spinal Injuries
To ensure that participants can demonstrate how to properly handle the victim of a suspected spinal injury in the water

Activity Point out and discuss the possible locations in the water where a spinal injury could occur. Explain possible ways of preventing such accidents. Discuss the different procedures that might be followed in various circumstances.

In shallow water, demonstrate and practice the following techniques: hip and shoulder support, the head splint, and the head/chin support, including rotating a facedown victim faceup. Demonstrate and practice the procedures for positioning a backboard under a victim, placing a cervical collar, securing the victim to the board, and removing the victim from the water.

Demonstrate and practice the techniques as described for use in deep water. Have the class practice spinal injury management techniques as a group, with participants taking turns in different roles, such as victim, initial rescuer, and so on.

Note: Safety measures for this practice session should include the following:

106

- Have at least one or two additional persons (lifeguards, assistant instructors, or aides) available to help in case of an emergency.
- Have a system for quickly removing the victim from the board (e.g., self-adhesive straps, or scissors for cutting the cravats).

Shallow Water

Suggested Time

1 hour, 10 minutes

Activity

Hip and Shoulder Support—Use in calm, shallow water only for faceup victim, when no help is immediately available to assist in boarding.
- Stand facing victim's side.
- Lower yourself to chest depth.
- Slide one arm under victim's shoulders.
- Slide other arm under victim's hip bones and support victim.
- Do not lift victim. Maintain in horizontal position until help arrives.
- Reassure and comfort victim.

Head Splint—Use in calm or choppy water, deep or shallow water, facedown victim.
- Stand facing victim's side.
- Gently bring victim's arms alongside the head, parallel to the surface, by grasping them midway between the elbow and the shoulder, right hand to right arm, left to left.
- Position the arms extended against victim's head.
- Apply pressure to the arms to splint the head, providing in-line stabilization.
- Lower your body to chest depth and move the victim slowly forward to a horizontal position, gliding victim to the surface.
- Once victim is horizontal, continue moving forward slowly and rotate victim toward you by pushing the arm closer to you

107

underwater while pulling victim's other arm across the surface to turn victim faceup. Lower your shoulders in the water as you do this.

- Rest victim's head in the crook of your arm but not **on** the arm.
- Maintain victim in a horizontal position until help arrives.

Head/Chin Support (for facedown or faceup victim)

- Approach from either side of victim.
- If necessary, move victim's arm that is nearer you to position victim's arm and shoulder against your chest.
- Lower your body until shoulders are at water level.
- Place your forearm along length of victim's breastbone, hand supporting victim's chin with thumb on one side, fingers on the other. Do not apply pressure yet.
- At the same time, place other forearm along length of victim's spine and position the hand to support victim's head at the base of the skull, thumb on one side, fingers on the other. Do not apply pressure yet.
- Lock both wrists and squeeze your forearms together. Apply pressure to the chin and the base of the skull. You are now providing in-line stabilization.
- Glide a facedown victim forward to horizontal position before turning victim.
- To turn victim faceup, rotate victim toward you.
- Submerge and go under victim as you turn victim faceup and surface on the other side. Move slowly to reduce any twisting to victim's body.
- Maintain victim in a horizontal position until help arrives.

- When sufficient help arrives, a second rescuer assists in providing in-line stabilization by placing both hands alongside victim's head.

Note: This technique can also be used with a submerged victim lying on his or her back, front, or side. Perform the steps just described and bring the victim to the surface at a 45-degree angle. Continue to use the head/chin support technique to move victim to shallow water.

Boarding Procedures
After stabilizing victim's head and neck by using any of the previously described techniques, place a backboard under the victim.
- Bring the backboard and approach victim from the side.
- Place backboard diagonally under victim from the side, foot end of the board going down in the water first.
- Hold board down under the water so as not to bump victim. Slide it under victim and position it lengthwise along victim's spine.
- Have board extend beyond victim's head near rescuer who is maintaining in-line stabilization.
- Allow board to rise under victim. At least one rescuer should be on each side of the board and one at victim's feet.
- Rescuer stabilizing victim's head and neck slowly and carefully withdraws his or her hands from victim's head as board is raised into place against victim.
- Second rescuer applies in-line stabilization.
- Initial rescuer applies appropriate-sized rigid cervical collar. Collar should fit securely, with victim's chin in proper

resting position and head maintained in neutral position by the collar.

- After collar is in place, secure victim's shoulders to the backboard by using straps or cravats. Criss-cross the chest with straps and secure at sides. Make sure straps are tight but not so tight as to restrict chest movement during normal breathing.
- Secure straps across hip bones.
- Secure hands alongside or in front of victim.
- Secure thighs and shins to board. If additional support is necessary, use figure-8 tie on ankles.
- Secure head. (Before securing victim's head to board, it may be necessary to place padding, such as a folded towel, under victim's head. The amount of padding needed will be evident from the space between the board and the head while in-line stabilization is maintained. Approximately one inch of padding is all that should be needed to keep head in neutral position. Caution participants **not** to lift or otherwise move victim's head while applying any necessary padding.)
- Place towel or blanket roll in horseshoe configuration around victim's neck and head.
- Secure forehead.

Note: Alternate methods of strapping may be used provided the technique meets the objectives for immobilizing the spine.

Removal From Water
- If in pool, move victim to side of pool.
- Position board perpendicular to the side of the pool.
- Remove board headfirst.

- Keep board horizontal as long as possible while it is being removed from the pool.
- Other rescuers on deck or dock help lift and slide board onto pool deck.
- Remove board and victim slowly and carefully.
- Give victim care for shock.
- Continue to monitor victim's level of consciousness and breathing.

Deep Water

Suggested Time

30 minutes

Note: Remind participants that people rarely suffer spinal injury in deep water. If this occurs, however, move victim to shallow water, if possible. If it is impossible to move victim into shallow water, swim fins are helpful in allowing a lifeguard to support a deep water victim of a suspected spinal injury until additional help arrives. At least five additional rescuers are necessary for deep water support. Explain that the following techniques for immobilizing a victim of a suspected spinal injury are used specifically in deep water.

Head Splint
- Keep victim afloat, as in shallow water support.
- Initial rescuer maintains head splint using victim's arms.
- If rescuer cannot swim to shallow water with victim, initial rescuer maintains head splint and swims to a corner of the pool or a ladder area where another rescuer can assist in supporting initial rescuer and victim.
- Once additional rescuers are available, one additional rescuer holds victim's feet at the

surface while one or two other rescuers place backboard under victim.
- Another rescuer lies or kneels on deck and supplies in-line stabilization.
- Initial rescuer releases victim's arms as other rescuers move board upward.
- The victim's arms are positioned gently at his or her sides.
- Place the cervical collar. Then strap victim and remove board from the water.

Head/Chin Support
- Turn victim, or place the hands properly for head/chin support if victim is faceup.
- Tread water with fins or swim in wide circles with victim until help arrives. If platform or similar device is available, use it.
- When help arrives, swim with victim to closest corner of pool or pool ladder. If using pool ladder, put one foot on one of the steps.
- Once additional rescuers are available, one should hold victim's feet while one or two other rescuers place the backboard under the victim.
- Another rescuer lies or kneels on the deck and applies in-line stabilization.
- As the backboard is moved up, the initial rescuer withdraws his or her arms.
- Rescuers place cervical collar on victim, then begin strapping.

Conditioning Swim

Suggested Time   20 minutes

Objective   To develop participants' strength and endurance in swimming and lifeguarding skills

Activity   Have participants work in pairs to practice the use of rescue buoys, rescue tubes, and rescue boards for swimming rescues and rescue breathing.

Review and Assignment

Suggested Time   5 minutes

Objective   To ensure participants' understanding of information covered to this point in the course

Activity   Review the key points of the session. Answer any questions that participants may have at this time. Give the following reading assignment:
- Textbook: Chapter 7, pages 7-8 and 7-9; Chapter 9, pages 9-15 through 9-18; Chapters 10, 11, and 12
- *Supplement:* Chapter 2

Session 8

Time	Approximately 3 hours
Topics	Search and Recovery Equipment and Operations; Weather and Environmental Conditions; Waterfront Areas; Use of Mask, Snorkel, and Fins
References	Textbook: Chapter 7, pages 7-8 and 7-9; Chapter 9, pages 9-15 through 9-18; Chapters 10, 11, and 12; *Supplement*: Chapter 2
Materials and Equipment	Chalkboard and chalk, or flip chart and markers; masks, fins, and snorkels; a canoe, row-boat, or other rescue boat (optional); buoyancy compensating devices (BCDs); divers' weight belts; appropriate audiovisual equipment (optional)
Facilities	Classroom and a pool or lake
Suggested Audiovisual	*Snorkeling Skills and Rescue Techniques,* 13 minutes

Review

Suggested Time	5 minutes
Objective	To verify participants' understanding of the information from the previous session
Activity	Review the accomplishments and objectives of the previous session. Allow participants to bring up topics for discussion that relate to the course content.

Search and Recovery Equipment and Operations

Suggested Time 20 minutes

Objective To ensure that participants become familiar with procedures for search and recovery operations and the equipment used in these operations

Activity

Search and Recovery Equipment

Refer participants to the textbook, pages 7-8 and 7-9.

Very briefly discuss the pieces of search and recovery equipment. Remind participants of the need for proper training in the use of this equipment.

- **Swim Fins**—Useful in rescues in open water areas when lifeguards must swim great distances for rescues, or when lifeguards have to dive to the bottom of a diving well. They can provide stabilization for a lifeguard attempting to give rescue breathing or supporting the victim of a spinal injury while in deep water. They are effective in search and recovery operations in open water. Made of rigid or semirigid rubber.
- **Face Mask**—Must have a shatterproof, tempered safety glass faceplate and a soft, flexible rubber skirt with a corrosion-proof metal or plastic reinforcement band.
- **Snorkel**—A hollow rubber tube 12 to 15 inches in length, with a soft rubber mouthpiece. The longer end of the tube must be open at all times.
- **Grappling Iron**—Size will be determined by the type of bottom (smooth, rocky, or overgrown with weeds).

116

- **Grappling Pole**—Used where the bottom is grassy or is littered with debris or tree stumps. A pole is usually 12 to 16 feet long with a barbless hook at one end.
- **Grappling Line**—A large pointed hook that is attached to one end of a line. It can be used in narrow, deep channels or in small areas between docks.

Point out that the use of certain search and recovery equipment, such as scuba equipment, vehicles, and aircraft, will be based on the type, location, and size of the facility.

Refer participants to the textbook, Chapter 10.

Discuss the need for organized search and recovery operations. Stress that the critical factor is speed. The victim must be found as quickly as possible.

Introduce the following guidelines to be used as a basis for organizing search and recovery operations. Point out that these guidelines can be modified to meet the needs of different facilities.

Organization, Planning, and Training
- Point out that all possible situations, such as a lost bather, a drowning, or a capsized boat, should be considered when developing plans for search and recovery operations.
- Stress the involvement of support personnel, such as police, fire, and EMS personnel, during the planning phase.
- Point out that a communications system must be established in order to keep all personnel informed during an emergency operation. Discuss the following situations that will require signals:
— Missing person

- — Referring facility staff to a designated area
- — Clearing the water, if necessary
- — Summoning additional staff or volunteers
- — Sounding "all clear"
- Emphasize that crowd control is essential to allow search and recovery operations to function properly.
- Point out that practice sessions should be scheduled regularly.
- Stress that support personnel should be involved as often as possible.
- Emphasize that records and evaluations should be kept on all practice sessions.

Operations

Activity

Discuss the following factors that must be considered when deciding the procedures to follow:
- Size and shape of the facility
- Condition of the bottom
- Absence or presence of a current
- Number of staff on duty
- Victim's age, skill level, and physical size
- Length of time the person has been missing
- Location where the person was last seen
- Number of patrons at the facility

Refer participants to the suggested procedure for a missing-person drill on pages 10-2 and 10-3 of the textbook. Remind participants that this procedure may be modified as appropriate for different facilities. Briefly discuss each of the 13 steps in a missing-person drill.

Briefly explain and discuss the following areas and formations for underwater search. Refer participants to pages 10-3 through 10-5 in the textbook.
- Shallow water areas—line formation

- Deep water areas—line, circle, half-circle formations.

Emphasize the safety of the searchers during all search and recovery operations.

Briefly discuss recovery operations, pages 10-5 through 10-7 in the textbook.

Note: The length of time for discussion on this subject will vary with the type and size of the facility where the course is being conducted.

Scuba
Emphasize that all personnel using scuba equipment must be trained and certified.

Weather and Environmental Conditions

Suggested Time

10 minutes

Objective

To ensure that participants will be able to describe various weather conditions and their effects on activities at aquatic facilities

Activity

Refer participants to the textbook, pages 11-1 to 11-4.

Explain and discuss the need for lifeguards to evaluate weather and environmental conditions as they relate to the safety of the patrons at an aquatic facility.

Point out the importance of weather and environmental agencies as a source of information. Discuss the following:
- Cloud formations
- Estimating distances to storms

Discuss procedures for removing patrons from the water because of an impending storm. Have participants tell you further safety precautions, such as those given on pages 11-2 and 11-3. Emphasize safety throughout the discussion.

Discuss with participants additional weather hazards that affect activity at aquatic facilities and the cautions and procedures lifeguards should take in the event of each.

- Heavy rains and hailstorms can cause dangerous conditions; heavy rains can affect water clarity.
- Tornadoes require two types of warnings.
  — Tornado watch: Tornadoes and thunderstorms are possible.
  — Tornado warning: A tornado has been sighted, take shelter.
- High temperatures can cause overcrowding in some areas of the facility. Emphasize that lifeguards must take precautions to guard against sunburn, heatstroke, and heat exhaustion.
- High winds can reduce visibility and influence currents. At waterfront and small craft areas, winds can determine the positioning of rescue boats. Winds may also restrict activity.
- Fog can cause a facility to close if visibility is limited.

Briefly discuss other environmental conditions that can cause hazardous conditions, such as submerged rocks and tree stumps, discoloration and turbidity of the water, and changes in bottom and shoreline conditions.

Waterfront Areas

**Suggested
Time**   20 minutes

Objective   To introduce participants to the characteristics of waterfront facilities

Activity	Refer participants to the textbook, pages 12-1 to 12-8.

Operational Procedures

Activity Explain and discuss the factors to be considered when establishing operational procedures at waterfront facilities.

- Natural features—terrain, source of water
- Water characteristics—currents
- Vantage points—influence of wind and sun on locations of lifeguards
- Types of activity—how to use all available space and still provide proper supervision
- Communications—effective systems with trained personnel
- Types and number of people—established capacity limits and screening procedures
- Times of greatest activity—times identified and proper supervision provided
- Availability of additional personnel—support personnel may be needed, some can be trained as instructor aides

Waterfront Characteristics

Activity Discuss with participants the following characteristics of a safe waterfront facility:

- General characteristics
  - Bottom: Gentle slope, no holes or drop-offs, free of obstructions
  - Swimming areas: Clearly identified and separated
  - Small craft areas: Clearly identified on the surface and underwater, if possible
  - Diving areas: Proper depths and clear identification for safe and unsafe areas
  - Beach areas: Clean and well maintained, proper drainage
  - Docks and floats: Anchored, proper supervision
  - Bathhouse: Cleaned daily, proper drainage

121

- Lifeguard stations
  —Towers: Elevated, provide clear views of area
  —Chairs or stands: Equipped with rescue equipment
  —Rescue boat: Separate boat for small craft area
- First aid station: Properly equipped and clearly identified

Counselors and Lookouts

Activity

Remind participants that support personnel can assist in the supervision of a swimming area.

Classification of Bathers and Boaters

Activity

Emphasize the safety advantages of bather classification.

Contour and Terrain Chart

Activity

Point out that these charts can be used to indicate environmental changes at the facility. Refer participants to Fig. 12-2 in the textbook.

Small Craft Safety

Activity

Emphasize the use of PFDs and signal flags as preventive actions. Remind participants of the importance of maintaining equipment in good working order.

Dock Formations and Rescue Boat Locations

Activity

Refer participants to Figs. 12-4 to 12-10 in the textbook. Remind participants that factors such as currents and wind direction will influence the location of docks and rescue boats.

Emphasize that dock formations shown in the textbook may be different at different facilities.

Break

Suggested Time   10 minutes

Activity   Participants should change clothes and prepare for the in-water skills practice.

Suggested Audiovisual   *Snorkeling Skills and Rescue Techniques,* 13 minutes

Skills Practice: Mask, Fins, and Snorkel; Entering the Water Wearing Snorkel Equipment; Swimming Wearing Snorkel Equipment; Search and Recovery Operations; Rescue of a Scuba Diver; Rescue Boats (optional)

Objective   To ensure that participants can demonstrate proper use of a mask, fins, and snorkel, and search and recovery techniques

Mask, Fins, and Snorkel

Suggested Time   35 minutes

Refer participants to the *Supplement,* Chapter 2

Activity   **Characteristics of Masks**
Display a swim mask and point out its features.
- Made of soft, flexible rubber
- Untinted, tempered safety glass faceplate
- Noncorrosive metal or plastic band
- Easily adjusted head strap
    If masks are available with purge valve and molded nose, point out these features also.

123

Defogging the Faceplate

Demonstrate and have participants practice defogging the faceplate:

- Prevent condensation from forming by rubbing inside of glass with commercially produced defogging agent or saliva.

Proper Mask Fitting

Point out that an important feature of a swim mask is proper fit.

- The mask must fit so that it seals properly against the face.
- The strap must be adjusted to fit the head comfortably but snugly.

Demonstrate how to test a mask for proper fit.

- Place mask against face without using the strap. (Keep your hair out of the way.)
- Inhale through nose. An airtight mask will stay in place without being held.
- Adjust strap to hold mask in place.
- Try on mask with face in the water.
- If it leaks, tighten strap.

Have participants test their masks for proper fit. Check each one to be sure it fits properly.

Clearing a Mask of Water

Explain that small amounts of water leak into a mask even with proper fit. Some masks have purge valves that let air and water out when you exhale. Masks without valves can also be emptied, or purged, while swimming without resurfacing.

In shallow water, demonstrate and have participants practice clearing a mask of water.

- Submerge in a sitting position and flood mask by lifting or tilting mask away from face, slowly allowing water to enter.
- Surface and stand up, taking a breath through your mouth.

- Tilt your head back slightly.
- Place two or three fingers or palm of hand on top of faceplate, press in against your forehead, and exhale forcefully through your nose, forcing water out under lower edge. (If the mask has a purge valve, tip head forward. If the mask does not have a purge valve, tip head backwards.)

Have participants repeat the procedure underwater in shallow water several times until they are comfortable with it.

Demonstrate and have participants practice purging a mask while swimming face-down in deep water.
- Turn head to either side (or turn on your side) and press with palm or two or three fingers on what was side of mask but is now top.
- Press firmly, exhale through nose, forcing out water.
- If mask has a purge valve, blow forcefully through nose to force water out the one-way valve.

Note. Lifeguards will generally surface, empty water out of the mask, and surface dive again because this is faster and easier, and the lifeguard has a limited supply of air in the lungs.

Relieving Mask and Ear Pressure
Explain that mask and ear pressure increases as a diver descends and can cause pain and possible injury.

Demonstrate and have participants practice relieving mask pressure.
- Exhale a little air through the nose into mask.

Demonstrate and have participants practice relieving ear pressure.

- Place thumb against bottom of mask and press mask against nostrils.
- Attempt to exhale through nose, or swallow.
- If mask has molded nose, use it to pinch nostrils shut while attempting to exhale through nose.

Types of Fins

Discuss the two basic types of fins: full foot or shoe-fin, and open-heel fin. Tell participants that fins must fit well or they will chafe the feet.

Walking With Fins

Demonstrate and have participants practice putting on and walking with fins.
- Wet both feet and fins before putting on.
- Walk backwards or sideways to avoid tripping, and look behind you or to the side.

Kicking With Fins

Demonstrate and have participants practice—
- Modified flutter kick.
  —Kicking action deeper and slower than flutter kick.
  —Greater knee bend.
- Dolphin kick.
  —Keep legs together.
  —Bend knees to bring fins up.
  —Arch back.
  —Straighten legs, bend forward at waist to bring legs down for power stroke.
  —Bend knees, brings fins up, and straighten body, then arch back and repeat motion.

Characteristics of Snorkels

Discuss the characteristics of a snorkel, using one or more snorkels for illustration:

- J-shaped, L-shaped, or flexible I-shaped rubber silicone tube, 3/4-inch in diameter, 12 to 15 inches long.
- May have straight or flared top.
- Should have soft mouthpiece with fluorescent safety band around top of barrel.
- Attaches to mask strap with snorkel keeper (small piece of rubber or plastic).

Using the Snorkel

Demonstrate and have participants practice putting a snorkel on and breathing through it.

- Secure snorkel to mask with snorkel keeper.
- Place mask on face and snorkel in mouth.
- Adjust position of snorkel in keeper and mask strap.
- Seal snorkel by holding lips tightly around the barrel.

Have participants practice breathing with their faces out of water until they are comfortable.

Clearing the Snorkel

Explain that water in the snorkel is a common occurrence, both from diving and from splashing at the surface. The swimmer should be able to clear water from the snorkel.

In shallow water, demonstrate and have participants practice flooding and clearing a snorkel.

- Take a breath.
- Submerge deep enough to flood snorkel.
- Return to surface, but with face submerged.
- Force water from snorkel by exhaling forcefully through tube.
- Inhale carefully and slowly in case any water remains in the tube. If some water remains in snorkel, exhale again.

Entering the Water Wearing Snorkeling Equipment

Suggested Time

20 minutes

Activity

Stride-Jump Entry

Demonstrate and have participants practice entering the water using a stride jump. Water should be at least 5 feet deep.
- Pull on fins and mask.
- Hold mask firmly with one hand covering faceplate.
- Keep elbow of that hand close to chest.
- Keep other arm extended down and forward.
- Take long stride over the water.
- When fins touch surface, quickly bring legs together with toes pointed to stop downward motion before head and shoulders are submerged.

Sit-In

From a deck or dock, demonstrate and have participants practice entering the water using a sit-in entry.
- Pull fins on.
- Put mask on and hold firmly with one hand covering the faceplate, elbows close to the chest.
- Place other hand at side.
- If standing, place heels even with edge of pool, back to the water.
- Then tuck chin on chest, pike at hips, and sit into the water, keeping legs straight.
- If entering from boat, sit on side with back to the water and hold on with one hand, holding mask with other hand.
- Tuck chin on chest and lean into water.

Do not use this entry if you are more than 2 feet above the water or water depth is less than 8 feet.

Swimming Wearing Snorkeling Equipment

Suggested Time

15 minutes

Activity

Surface Diving and Resurfacing
Demonstrate how to perform a surface dive and resurface:
- Roll forward into tuck or pike position.
- Stop, look, and listen on returning to surface.
- Extend a hand overhead before surfacing.
- Upon reaching the surface, clear snorkel and resume normal breathing.

Swimming Underwater
Explain, demonstrate, and have participants practice swimming underwater while wearing fins, using legs only.

Search and Recovery Operations

Suggested Time

15 minutes

Objective

To ensure that participants can demonstrate search and recovery procedures

Activity

Explain, demonstrate, and practice the procedures and patterns for search and recovery operations. Provide for the safety of participants.

Note: If the course is confined to a pool, dive to the maximum depth of the pool, but no deeper than 12 feet. In an open-water facility, dive to a maximum depth of 12 feet. Potential lifeguards should know that they may be required by their future employer to be able to dive to a depth greater than 12 feet. Review relieving ear pressure. Demonstrate clearing the inner ear canal by pinching the nose and attempting to blow the nose to equalize pressure. Have the participants practice.

During practice sessions, concentrate on organization and communication. Emphasize (1) the need for speed in an actual emergency, (2) that the legs provide most of the underwater propulsion, (3) that arms and hands should sweep slowly underwater, and (4) that slow movements of arms and legs help to prevent stirring up sand or silt on the bottom.
- Shallow water areas
  —Line formation
- Deep water areas
  —Line formation
  —Full-circle formation
  —Half-circle formation
- At open-water facilities, demonstrate and practice grappling operations if time permits or schedule additional time.
  —Single boat
  —Dock-to-dock
  —Boat-to-shore

Rescue of a Scuba Diver

Suggested Time

10 minutes

Objective

To enable participants to become familiar with the skills required for rescuing a scuba diver

Activity

Explain and discuss the rescue of a scuba diver. Explain to participants that the latest technology regarding rescue of a scuba diver reverses the "Breathe" and "Inflate" steps in the rescue procedures given in the textbook on page 9-16. Ask participants to mark their textbooks accordingly, putting the "Inflate" step before "Breathe."

Note: Demonstrations and practice of proper hand positioning on a victim wearing full scuba gear must be restricted to the deck or to the beach areas.

Review and discuss the following procedures for rescuing a scuba diver.
- Release the weight belt.
- Maintain an open airway for the victim.
- Bring the victim to the surface, slowly.
- Inflate the diver's BCD.
- Give two slow breaths.

If possible, several types of BCDs and diver's weight belts should be shown and demonstrated for participants. Emphasize that participants should be familiar with the various types of equipment that may be used at the facility where they will be working. Refer participants to page 9-16 in the textbook.

Briefly discuss with participants the uses of Surface-Air-Supplied equipment. Emphasize the need for them to become familiar with any SAS equipment at their facility. Refer participants to page 9-11 in the textbook.

Rescue Boats

Suggested Time

15 minutes (optional)

Objective

To increase the participants' skills in handling small craft during rescue operations

Note: If this skill practice is being conducted at a pool facility, it will be necessary to emphasize procedures to prevent craft from hitting the sides of the pool. The use of bow and stern lines or fenders is recommended. Participants should practice approaching and rescuing both a distress victim and a drowning victim.

If this skill practice is being conducted at a waterfront facility, schedule additional time to allow participants to develop and improve personal skill in handling small craft and rescue operations.

Activity

Small Craft Safety
Demonstrate and discuss small craft safety and tell participants that small craft accidents are most likely to occur when—
- Entering or leaving craft from shore or dock
- Assisting passengers in and out
- Exchanging positions
- Entering from deep water
- Righting and entering capsized craft

Use of Small Craft for Rescue of Tired Swimmer
Demonstrate and practice the proper techniques for using rescue boats:
- Approaching victim with boat
- Extending equipment to victim
- Stabilizing victim in the water while he or she is holding on to the side of the craft
- Administering rescue breathing (mouth-to-mouth resuscitation) over the side of the boat with the victim in the water

Emphasize safety for both the victim and the lifeguard.

Conditioning Swim

Suggested Time

15 minutes

Activity

Review caring for spinal injuries by turning, boarding, and removing a victim from the water.

Review

**Suggested
Time**   5 minutes

Objective   To ensure that participants understand the
information covered thus far in the course

Activity   Review the key points of the session. Answer
any questions participants might have. Tell
participants that the last two sessions will
consist of the written examination, skills
testing, and graduation. Tell students to come
to Session 9 dressed for the final skills test but
to bring dry clothes for the second part of the
session, which will review the content of the
course.

Session 9

Time	Approximately 2 hours, 25 minutes
Topics	Written Examination; Final Skills Test and Practice, Part 1.
References	Textbook and *Supplement*
Materials and Equipment	Chalkboard and chalk, or flip chart and markers; diving bricks
Facilities	Classroom and a pool or lake

Review

Suggested Time	30 minutes
Objective	To verify participants' understanding of the information covered in the course
Activity	Review the objectives and content of the previous sessions. Allow participants to bring up topics for discussion that relate to the material.

Written Examination

Suggested Time	40 minutes
Objective	To test each participant's knowledge of the information contained in the course

Activity   Administer a 40-question written examination, selected from the bank of 60 questions, which covers material from reading assignments and class presentations.

Ask the participants to complete the Participant Course Evaluation (Appendix G). Give the form to each participant when he or she completes the written examination. Ask the participants to leave the completed evaluations in a box or envelope you have placed on a desk or table near the door.

Break

**Suggested
Time**   10 minutes

Activity   Participants should change clothes and prepare for the in-water skills practice.

Final Skills Test

**Suggested
Time**   1 hour

Objective   To evaluate each participant's performance of rescue skills

Activity   Explain the testing procedures and events to the participants. Clarify any areas of misunderstanding and highlight the key points of performing each skill.

Remind participants that all skills must be performed satisfactorily to pass the test and the course.

1. Participant will perform a stride jump into deep water at least 9 feet deep, approach swim 15 yards to an unconscious victim; perform a front surface approach; position the victim for a wrist tow; and tow

the victim to the starting position in the water.

2. From a deck or dock, participant will dive into water at least 9 feet deep and execute a dive to the rear to approach an active nonstruggling victim; position the victim in either a single or double armpit tow; and tow the victim to the starting position in the water.

3. Participant will jump into deep water (at least 9 feet) from the pool deck or a dock, using a rear approach to an active victim; contact the victim and level him or her using a single or double armpit tow; and then position the victim in a cross-chest or alternate cross-chest carry and return to the starting point. *Note:* The distance from the rescuer to the victim should be 15 yards.

4. Participant will tread water for 1 minute holding a diving brick at the surface with both hands.

5. The participant will demonstrate his or her ability to execute the following skills:
   a. One- and two-hand block
   b. Wrist-grip escape
   c. Rear head-hold escape
   d. Front head-hold escape

Assignment

Suggested Time   5 minutes

Objective   To prepare participants for the final skills test

Activity   Explain how the final swim test will be administered. The sequence of events, timing procedures, and evaluation procedures should be clarified at this time. Tell participants to come to Session 10 wearing swimsuits for the final skills test.

Session 10

Time	Approximately 1 hour, 35 minutes
Topics	Review of Written Examination, Final Skills Test, Part 2
Reference	Textbook and *Supplement*
Materials and Equipment	Diving bricks and a stopwatch, two rescue tubes
Facilities	A pool or lake
Suggested Audiovisual	*Emergency Aquatic Skills*: Unit 10—*Review and Closing*, 3 minutes

Review of Written Examination

Suggested Time	15 minutes
Objective	To verify understanding of the information contained in the written examination
Activity	Return the graded tests to the participants. Clarify any misunderstandings that participants may have at this point and/or refer participants to the textbook. Collect the examinations at the end of the discussion. The number of participants who missed each question should be tabulated. This will help in the evaluation of the test and the instructor's teaching.

Final Skills Test

Suggested Time   1 hour

Objective   To evaluate each participant's performance of swimming and rescue skills

Activity   Explain the testing procedures and events to the participants. Clarify any areas of misunderstanding about how the test is conducted.

Remind participants that all skills must be performed satisfactorily to pass the test and in the order given here.

The skills and swimming test is made up of the following events:

1. Participant will perform a shallow dive into deep water and swim an approach stroke 25 yards in 18 seconds or less.

2. Participant will enter shallow water (ease in) and approach a victim who is facedown on the surface simulating a spinal injury. Participant will properly turn the victim to a faceup position and support the victim at the surface.

3. Participant will enter deep water (ease in) and approach a victim who is floating facedown on the surface simulating a spinal injury. Participant will turn the victim properly and while maintaining contact, swim the victim to a corner of the pool or the shallow end.

4. Participant will make a shallow dive, approach 10 yards, surface dive 9 feet, bring a 10-pound diving brick from the bottom to the surface in 11 seconds from the time the participant dives in until the participant's head breaks the surface. *Note:* To compensate for varying pool depths, add 1 second to the time for each foot of water over 9 feet.

140

5. Participant will swim with rescue tube 20 yards to passive victim, approach, wrap tube around victim, and tow victim back to safety while simulating rescue breathing.
6. Participant will perform a shallow dive, sprint 25 yards, recover a diving brick from a pool gutter or edge, and carry the brick back 25 yards, all in 1 minute, 10 seconds or less.

Review and Summary

Suggested Time   20 minutes

Objective   To ensure an understanding of the material covered in the course

Suggested Audiovisual   *Emergency Aquatic Skills*: Unit 10 — *Review and Closing*, 3 minutes

Activity   Review the objectives of this session and all previous sessions. Answer any questions that participants may have concerning the material.

Give a general assessment of the total group's progress in skill development.

Emphasize the importance of recognizing the responsibility an individual assumes as a lifeguard.

Inform participants of other Red Cross courses that are available. Stress the importance of further training.

Present course completion certificates to participants who have completed the course. Have extra emblems and pins available for participants to purchase.

Prepare the *Course Record* (Form 6418) and *Course Record Addendum* (Form 6418A) for submission to your Red Cross chapter.

Fill out a copy of the Instructor Course Evaluation (Appendix H) and mail it to the address given on the Evaluation (first and fourth times you teach the course).

Appendix A

Sample Letter to Participants

On the following page is a sample letter that might be sent to class participants to confirm registration and to give them important information about the course.

Date:___/___/___

Dear Course Participant,

Thank you for enrolling in an American Red Cross Lifeguard Training course. The time and place of the class meetings are listed below.

Course Name (specify): _____

Date(s): _____

Time: _____

Place: _____

Directions (if needed): _____

_____

_____

In this course, you will learn about the duties and responsibilities of a lifeguard and how to carry them out. You will also learn a number of lifeguarding techniques, such as how to tow or carry a victim to safety, how to manage a suspected spinal injury in the water, and how to use rescue equipment to help rescue a distressed or drowning victim.

These practices require strenuous activity. If you have a medical condition or disability that might prevent you from taking part in the practice sessions, or if you have any questions at all about your ability to fully participate in lifeguard training, you should discuss it with the appropriate person at your local chapter or unit.

To enroll in the Lifeguard Training course, you must be at least 15 years old. You must also pass a skills test, given in the first session of the course, requiring you to perform the following skills:

- Swim 500 yards continuously using each of the following strokes for at least 50 yards: crawl, breaststroke, elementary backstroke, sidestroke.
- Surface dive to a minimum depth of 9 feet and bring a 10-pound diving brick to the surface
- Surface dive to a minimum depth of 5 feet and swim underwater for a minimum of 15 yards.
- Tread water for one minute.

You must also have a current (within 3 years) American Red Cross Standard First Aid certificate (or equivalent) and a current (within 1 year) American Red Cross Adult CPR certificate (or equivalent) or acquire them before graduating from the Lifeguard Training course.

Appendix B

Equipment and Supplies

Required Materials for Participants

❑ *American Red Cross Lifeguard Training* textbook
   (Stock No. 321119)

❑ *American Red Cross Lifeguard Training Supplement*
   (Stock No. 329448)

❑ A notebook and a pen or pencil

❑ A bathing suit and towel (for every session)

❑ A face mask, swim fins, and a snorkel (It may be that some
   participants will be unable to provide this equipment. Instructors
   may have to work out sharing arrangements or rent equipment from
   scuba diving shops. Some facilities may be able to provide certain
   items.)

Equipment Required for the Course
(The number in parentheses after each item indicates the number
required for a class of ten participants.)

❑ *American Red Cross Lifeguard Training* textbook (10)

❑ *American Red Cross Lifeguard Training Supplement* (10)

❑ Lifeguard Training course written tests and answer sheets (10)

❑ Shepherd's crook and/or reaching pole (2)

❑ Heaving line (2)

❑ Ring buoy, heaving jug, or throw bag (2)

❑ Rescue tube or rescue buoy (3)

❑ Backboard and set (6 each) of straps and ties (2)

❑ Rigid cervical collar (2)

❑ Blanket (for backboard head collar) (2)

❑ Padding material (2 towels each) for backboard (2)

❑ Whistle (1)

- ❑ Set of three signal flags (1)

- ❑ Diving brick (2)

- ❑ Personal flotation devices (PFDs) (2)

- ❑ Rescue board or surfboard (2)

- ❑ Scuba weight belt, without weights (2)

- ❑ Stopwatch (minimum of 2 for final skills test)

Additional Equipment Required for Course at Waterfront Facility
- ❑ Rescue boat(s) and oars, or canoe(s) and paddles

Additional Equipment Required for Course at Pool
- ❑ Kits for testing chemical balance of water

Suggested Instructional Aids
- ❑ 16mm projector, screen, extension cord, take-up reel, and spare bulbs; or VHS-VCR and monitor

- ❑ Extra paper and pencils

- ❑ Chalkboard and chalk or similar items (such as a flip chart with easel and marking pens)

- ❑ List of rules and regulations, various emergency action plans, and records and reports from aquatic facilities.

Appendix C

Video Calibration Chart

Because there is no standard "counter" on VCR equipment, and because machines can vary slightly in playing speed, instructors may find it useful to fill out this chart prior to class. It will allow the instructor to locate specific segments of the video for viewing.

Instructions (prior to class):

1. Use the same VCR you will use during class.
2. Make sure the tape is completely rewound.
3. Set the VCR in the play mode.
4. As soon as the words "The programs of the American Red Cross are made possible by the voluntary services and financial support of the American people," appear on the screen, set the VCR counter to zero. (The button to set the counter to zero is often called "Reset.")
5. Enter the counter number at the start of each segment in the space provided below.

American Red Cross Emergency Aquatic Skills

Unit 1: *Introduction to the Program* .... _____
Unit 2: *Recognition of a Drowning Victim* .... _____
Unit 3: *Nonswimming Assists* .... _____
Unit 4: *Entries* .... _____
Unit 5: *Approaches* .... _____
Unit 6: *Swimming Assists and Tows* .... _____
Unit 7: *Removal From the Water* .... _____
Unit 8: *Defenses and Escapes* .... _____
Unit 9: *Advanced Rescue Skills* .... _____
Unit 10: *Review and Closing*.. _____

Appendix D

Lifeguarding Skills Checklist

On the following page is a copy of the form for the instructor to use in checking off participant's skills as they perform them correctly. The form is available from your local chapter.

American Red Cross
LIFEGUARDING SKILLS CHECKLIST

Check off the skills listed on the left in the boxes that are shaded **gray**.

Check off the skills listed on the right in the **unshaded** boxes.

	Tows and Carries						Removal From Water				Defense		Escapes and Maneuvers				
	Single Armpit	Double Armpit	Wrist	Change From Wrist to Armpit	Cross-Chest Carry	Alternate Cross-Chest Carry	Lift From Water	Shallow Water Assist	Beach Drag	Pack-Strap Carry	One-Hand Block	Two Hand Block	Swim With Victim Holding On	Front-Head Hold	Rear-Head Hold	Wrist-Grip	Multiple Near-Drowning Maneuver

Nonswimming Assists
- Reaching
- Equipment Extension
- Throwing

Entries
- Stride Jump
- Feetfirst
- Ease-in

Rescue Skills
- Beach
- Shallow Dive
- Approach Strokes
- Ready Position
- Rescue Kicks

Surface Dives
- Feetfirst
- Pike or Tuck

Approaches
- Quick
- Recovery of Submerged Victim
- Swim or Dive to Rear
- Front Surface

Assists
- Rear
- On Front/Back
- By Two Lifeguards

American Red Cross Form 6608

Checklists are not to be sent to chapter. Retain for own use.

LIFEGUARDING SKILLS CHECKLIST

	Spinal Injury—Shallow Water, Deep Water					Mask, Fins, and Snorkel						
	Hip and Shoulder Support	Head Splint	Head/Chin Support	Boarding	Removal From the Water	Fitting, Clearing (Mask)	Relieving Mask and Ear Pressure	Kicking (Fins)	Using, Clearing (Snorkel)	Entering Water (Snorkeling Equipment)	Swimming (Snorkeling Equipment)	Search and Recovery

Row labels:

Rescue Breathing
- Shallow Water
- Deep Water

Using Rescue Equipment
- Rescue Board—Tired Victim
- Rescue Board—Panicky Victim
- Rescue Tube—Throwing Assist
- Rescue Tube/Buoy—Stride Jump Entry
- Rescue Tube/Buoy—Beach Entry
- Rescue Tube—Around Victim

Rescue Equipment and Rescue Breathing
- Rescue Tube—Front Surface
- Rescue Tube—Block and Turn
- Rescue Tube—Rear Approach
- Rescue Tube—Straddle
- Rescue Buoy—Front Surface, Buoy to Back
- Rescue Buoy—Front Surface, Buoy to Side
- Rescue Buoy—Rear Approach
- Rescue Board

Patterns of Class Organization

Arranging the Class for a Discussion on Land

Formation: Semicircle (one or more lines)

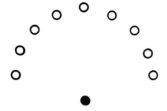

When Used   When speaking to the group

Important Factors

- The sun should be behind the participants.

- The group should face away from distracting influences.

- Wind coming from behind the instructor will help to carry his or her voice to the participants.

Arranging the Class for a Demonstration in the Water (Three Formations)

Formation: "L" (Single or Multiple Lines)

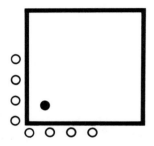

When Used   When the end and side of the pool or the dock are available

Important Factors
- The demonstrator should work directly in front of the participants.

- If talking against the wind, the demonstrator should talk toward the water and allow the sound to be carried over the water.

- Participants should be close enough to and high enough above the demonstrator so that they can look down at the demonstration.

Formation: Single Line

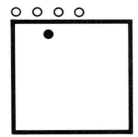

When Used When working from a bulkhead or from the side of the pool or the dock when the group is small

Important Factors
- The demonstrator should work directly in front of the participants.

- If talking against the wind, the demonstrator should talk toward the water and allow the sound to be carried over the water.

- Participants should be close enough to and high enough above the demonstrator so that they can look down at the demonstration.

Formation: Multiple Lines

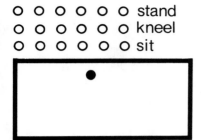

When Used When working from a bulkhead, or from the side of the pool or the dock when the group is large

Important Factors

- One group sits, the next group kneels, and the third group stands.

- The demonstrator should work directly in front of the participants.

- If talking against the wind, the demonstrator should talk toward the water and allow the sound to be carried over the water.

- Participants should be close enough to and high enough above the demonstrator so that they can look down at the demonstration.

Arranging the Class for Fluid Drills

Fluid drill formations are used to improve the skill efficiency and the physical endurance of the participants as well as to evaluate the participants. These drills should be varied to meet the needs of the participants and the instructor. The following factors should be considered when these drill formations are used:

- The participants' skill proficiency level

- Their physical condition

- The distance of each swim

- The intensity level of each swim

- The frequency and length of rest periods between swims

Formation: Wave

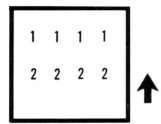

When Used
- To divide a large group into smaller units to provide maximum supervised participant practice

- To allow the instructor to observe fewer participants at one time in order to make comments for skill improvement

Important Factors
- The group is divided into smaller groups known as No. 1, No. 2, etc.

- The instructor must tell each group what to do and when to do it. *Example:* "Side stroke. No. 1's, ready; swim!"

- Each group swims as a unit on the appropriate command.

- Each group swims to a designated point and stops.

The wave formation is one of the most often used of all fluid drill formations. Consequently, the instructor should become skilled in organizing a class quickly.

- For fluid drills (and static drills) on dry land or in shallow water, have the participants line up in one straight line. Have them count off according to the number of groups desired.

- For fluid drills in deep water, have the participants line up by holding onto the edge of the pool or dock. Have them count off.

Formation: Stagger

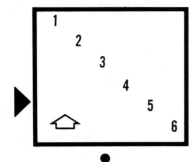

When Used   When it is necessary to watch participants individually and for final evaluation of many skills. The participants' safety is of primary importance.

Important Factors

- The group remains in a single line.

- Signal the first participant to start swimming. If two instructors are available, start each end of the line simultaneously.

- The participant next in line starts when the swimmer just ahead reaches the spot designated by the instructor.

- The instructor should be able to follow the progress of each participant for a few body lengths.

- The instructor usually moves along the deck in order to get a better view of the swimmers.

Formation: Short-Course or Long-Course Swim

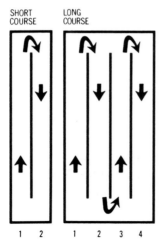

SHORT COURSE   LONG COURSE

1 2   1 2 3 4

When Used
- For practicing distance swimming in a long, narrow enclosed area

- For building participants' stamina and for permitting instructor to pay individual attention to the participants

Important Factors

- The swimming area is divided into smaller areas, with two lanes each for one or more areas (short course), or into multiple lanes (long course).

- For the short course, divide the group by the number of areas available. One group is assigned to each area, grouped by similar abilities if necessary.

- For the long course, place the faster swimmers ahead of the slower ones.

- Designate the number of laps (one length or width of the pool) to be completed before stopping.

- The swimmers should keep a safe distance apart.

Arranging the Class for Static Drills on Land or in Shallow Water

Formation: Single Line

OR

When Used When the area is long and narrow or the group is small, either on land or in the water

Important Factors
- The participants should be far enough apart so as not to interfere with each other.

- The instructor may stand in front of or at either end of the line.

Formation: Parallel Lines

OR

When Used When the area is long and narrow and the group is large

Important Factors
- Especially effective when the participants work in pairs.

- The instructor may stand in front of or at either end of the lines.

Formation: Multiple Lines

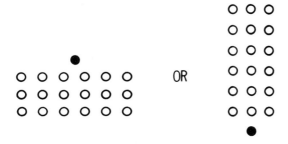

When Used   When the area is short and wide and the group is large

Important Factors
- The participants should be far enough apart so as not to interfere with each other.

- The instructor must be visible to all participants and must be able to see all participants.

Formation: Circle

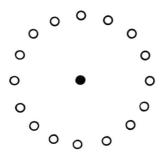

When Used
Important Factors

When the area is short and wide and the group is large
- It is difficult to observe all the participants at the same time with this formation.

- The instructor must be certain that all participants are able to see the demonstrations.

- The instructor should have a certified lifeguard outside of the circle for the safety of the participants, or the instructor must turn around frequently to observe the participants.

Formation: Semi-Circle

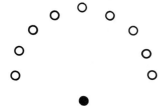

When Used When the area is limited in length and width and the group is small

Important Factors

- The sun should be behind the participants.

- The group should face away from distracting influences.

- Wind coming from behind the instructor will help to carry his or her voice to the participants.

Formation: "V" formation

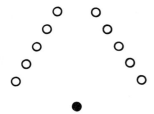

When Used When the area is limited in width

Important Factor

- The participants must be placed so as not to interfere with each other's vision or motion.

Appendix F

Guidelines for Conducting the Lifeguard Training Review Course

The American Red Cross Lifeguard Review Training course is based on competency and is self-paced. The first session of the course is a testing session. An individual who (1) passes a written test made up of 40 questions from the bank of 60 questions in the *Lifeguard Training Instructor Manual* with a score of 80 percent, (2) participates in a complete backboarding procedure for a victim of suspected spinal injury, and (3) passes all the final skills tests as given in this *Instructor's Manual* should receive a certificate at that time and not be required to take the Review course. The skills tests are listed in Sessions 9 and 10 of this manual and on the Final Skills Checklist (Appendix J). For 10 participants, this testing session may take approximately 3 and a half hours.

Eligibility Requirements

The participant must—
❑ Possess a current American Red Cross Lifeguard Training certificate.
❑ Possess a current American Red Cross Adult CPR certificate or equivalent.
❑ Possess a current American Red Cross Standard First Aid certificate or equivalent.
❑ Perform the following skills in a satisfactory manner:
  • Swim 500 yards continuously using one of the following strokes for at least 50 yards each: crawl, breaststroke, elementary backstroke, sidestroke.
  • Surface dive to a minimum of 9 feet and bring a 10-pound diving brick to the surface.
  • Surface dive to a minimum depth of 5 feet and swim underwater a minimum of 15 yards.
  • Tread water for 1 minute.
Note: Participants must be told that to receive a certificate they must pass both a written examination and a final skills test. Timed events and physical conditioning will be part of the course.

Course Length

The course takes approximately 9 hours to complete.

Course Requirements — Participant

Each participant is required to have—
- ❑ A copy of the *American Red Cross Lifeguard Training* textbook (Stock No. 321119).

- ❑ A copy of the *American Red Cross Lifeguard Training Supplement* (Stock No. 329448).

- ❑ Equipment as specified for the Lifeguard Training course.

Course Requirements — Instructor

The instructor must—
- ❑ Be a currently authorized American Red Cross Lifeguard Training instructor and should be experienced in teaching the Lifeguard Training course.

- ❑ Require that the participants attend all sessions.

- ❑ Review all skills learned in the Lifeguard Training course, and emphasize those skills tested in the final skills test.

- ❑ Require that the participants satisfactorily perform all skills in the Lifeguard Training course.

- ❑ Because of limited class time for discussion, hold the participants responsible for reviewing the contents of the *Lifeguard Training* textbook and the *Supplement* through reading assignments and homework.

Testing

The participants must pass the written examination with a minimum score of 80 percent and must pass the skills tests to complete the course satisfactorily. Testing is mandatory and consists of—
- ❑ A 40-question written examination.

- ❑ Skills tests as described in the *Lifeguard Training Instructor's Manual*.

Course Completion Certificate (Lifeguard Training)

Present course completion certificates to participants who have successfully completed this Lifeguard Training Review course. The certificate (C3416) is valid for three years from the date of issue.

Prepare *Course Record* (Form 6418) and *Course Record Addendum* (Form 6418A) for submission to your Red Cross chapter.

Lifeguard Training Review Course Outline

Session 1

Activity	Approximate Time
Introduce yourself; welcome participants, and check certificates.	5 minutes
Discuss course requirements and schedule.	10 minutes
Review emergency action plans.	45 minutes
Conduct skill screening.	40 minutes
Conduct a skills review: • Approaches, tows, and carries • Removal from the water • Defense and escapes	80 minutes
Session 1, Total Time	**3 hours**

Session 2

Activity	Approximate Time
Discuss spinal injury management show the video *Spinal Injury Mangement* (optional but strongly recommended).	30 minutes
Discuss legal liabilities.	30 minutes
Practice spinal injury mangement.	60 minutes
Review mask, fins, and snorkel.	30 minutes
Review other lifeguard skills of special interest to course participants.	30 minutes
Session 2, Total Time	**3 hours**

Session 3

Activity	Approximate Time
Administer the written test.	40 minutes
Correct the written test.	20 minutes
Administer the final skills test.	120 minutes
Session 3, Total Time	**3 hours**
Total course time	**9 hours**

Appendix G

American Red Cross Lifeguard Training Participant Course Evaluation

We would like to know what you thought about this American Red Cross Lifeguard Training course. You can help maintain the high quality of the course by completing this evaluation.

1. Tell us what you thought of the course. (Circle or check your choice.)

	Strongly Agree	Agree	Not Sure	Dis-agree	Strongly Disagree	Did Not Use
a. The textbook explained things clearly.	1	2	3	4	5	❑
b. The *Supplement* explained things clearly.	1	2	3	4	5	❑
c. The demonstrations in the audiovisuals were clear and helpful.	1	2	3	4	5	❑
d. I have confidence that I can do these skills correctly.	1	2	3	4	5	❑
e. The instructor was well prepared.	1	2	3	4	5	❑
f. The instructor gave clear instructions on what to do next.	1	2	3	4	5	❑
g. The instructor answered questions clearly.	1	2	3	4	5	❑
h. The instructor helped me during the practice sessions.	1	2	3	4	5	❑
i. I would recommend this course to a friend.	1	2	3	4	5	❑
j. I know when to use the skills I learned in this course.	1	2	3	4	5	❑
k. I had to work hard to pass this course.	1	2	3	4	5	❑

2. Was all the equipment in good order? ❑ Yes ❑ No
3. Was the classroom clean and comfortable? ❑ Yes ❑ No
4. Was the facility well suited to skills practice? ❑ Yes ❑ No
5. Did you have enough time to read? ❑ Yes ❑ No
6. Did you have enough time to practice? ❑ Yes ❑ No
7. Did you take this course to fulfill a job/work requirement? ❑ Yes ❑ No

If not, why did you take this course?

_____

_____

8. Did you learn what you wanted to learn?   ❑ Yes   ❑ No

   If yes, please specify:

_____

_____

If no, what else did you want to learn?

_____

_____

9. What was your age at your last birthday? _____

10. Please check the highest level of education you have completed.

    ❑ Elementary school   ❑ Junior high school   ❑ High school

    ❑ Some college   ❑ College degree or beyond

11. How did you hear about this course?

    ❑ Newspaper   ❑ Television   ❑ Radio

    ❑ Friend or relative   ❑ Employer   ❑ Pamphlet or poster

    ❑ Other (please specify): _____

12. Where do you expect to get a job as a lifeguard?

    ❑ Pool   ❑ Waterfront (lake)   ❑ Ocean beach

13. Are you:

    ❑ Male

    ❑ Female

14. Do you have any other comments about this course or your instructor that you would like to share with us?

_____

Thank you for answering these questions. We hope you enjoyed the course.

American Red Cross Lifeguard Training Instructor Course Evaluation

To continue to improve the Lifeguard Training course, the American Red Cross needs your help. Please complete a copy of this form the **FIRST** time you teach a Lifeguard Training course, and complete another copy the **FOURTH** time you teach it. Return the completed evaluations to:

> American Red Cross
> Programs and Services Department
> 17th and D Streets, N.W.
> Washington, DC 20006

Background

1. Today's date: ___/___/___/

2. Number of participants: ____

3. Is this your first or fourth time teaching the course?
    ❑ First   ❑ Fourth

4. What type of instructor are you?
    ❑ Red Cross volunteer
    ❑ Red Cross paid instructor
    ❑ Other (please specify): _____

5. Total time required to complete the course: ____ hours.

6. How would you describe the participants in this course?
    ❑ Mostly under age 18   ❑ Mostly ages 18 to 40
    ❑ Mostly ages 41 to 65   ❑ Mixed ages

7. Of these participants, how many expect to be lifeguards at
    ❑ Pool   ❑ Waterfront (lake)   ❑ Beach (ocean)

8. In what setting did you teach this course? (If at a pool facility, also check indoor or outdoor.)

    ❑ Public School Pool
    ❑ College/University Pool
    ❑ Community Pool
        ❑ Indoor   ❑ Outdoor
❑ Waterfront (Lake)
❑ Other (describe) _____

9. How long have you been an American Red Cross Lifeguard Training instructor? _____

10. When you taught this course, which of the following items did you use?

    ❑ Textbook   ❑ Audiovisuals
    ❑ *Supplement* ❑ Other items (describe):
    _____

Course

11. Do you have any questions about the course that are not answered in the *Instructor's Manual?*

12. Do you have any suggestions for improving the *Instructor's Manual?*

13. Do you have any suggestions for improving the textbook?

14. Do you have any suggestions for improving the *Supplement?*

15. Do you have any suggestions for improving the audiovisuals?

Optional: If you are willing to discuss your comments with us, please give us your name and a daytime phone number. We would like to be able to call you if we have any questions.

Name _____ Phone number (_____)_____

Chapter name _____

Thank you for taking the time to answer these questions. If you have any additional comments about the course, please include them on a separate sheet and attach it to this evaluation.

Appendix H

American Red Cross Lifeguard Training Instructor Course Evaluation

To continue to improve the Lifeguard Training course, the American Red Cross needs your help. Please complete a copy of this form the **FIRST** time you teach a Lifeguard Training course, and complete another copy the **FOURTH** time you teach it. Return the completed evaluations to:

American Red Cross
Programs and Services Department
17th and D Streets, N.W.
Washington, DC 20006

Background

1. Today's date: ___/___/___/

2. Number of participants: ____

3. Is this your first or fourth time teaching the course?
   ❑ First   ❑ Fourth

4. What type of instructor are you?
   ❑ Red Cross volunteer
   ❑ Red Cross paid instructor
   ❑ Other (please specify): _____

5. Total time required to complete the course: ____ hours.

6. How would you describe the participants in this course?
   ❑ Mostly under age 18   ❑ Mostly ages 18 to 40
   ❑ Mostly ages 41 to 65   ❑ Mixed ages

7. Of these participants, how many expect to be lifeguards at
   ❑ Pool   ❑ Waterfront (lake)   ❑ Beach (ocean)

8. In what setting did you teach this course? (If at a pool facility, also check indoor or outdoor.)
- ❑ Public School Pool
- ❑ College/University Pool
- ❑ Community Pool
  - ❑ Indoor   ❑ Outdoor
- ❑ Waterfront (Lake)
- ❑ Other (describe) _____

9. How long have you been an American Red Cross Lifeguard Training instructor? _____

10. When you taught this course, which of the following items did you use?
- ❑ Textbook   ❑ Audiovisuals
- ❑ *Supplement*   ❑ Other items (describe):
_____

Course

11. Do you have any questions about the course that are not answered in the *Instructor's Manual*?

12. Do you have any suggestions for improving the *Instructor's Manual?*

13. Do you have any suggestions for improving the textbook?

14. Do you have any suggestions for improving the *Supplement*?

15. Do you have any suggestions for improving the audiovisuals?

Optional: If you are willing to discuss your comments with us, please give us your name and a daytime phone number. We would like to be able to call you if we have any questions.

Name _____ Phone number (_____)_____

Chapter name _____

Thank you for taking the time to answer these questions. If you have any additional comments about the course, please include them on a separate sheet and attach it to this evaluation.

Appendix I

American Red Cross Lifeguard Training Test Questions

The following pages contain 60 test questions divided into four groups. The number in parentheses tells the chapter in the *Lifeguard Training* textbook to which the content of the question refers. The letter S. and a number in parentheses indicates the chapter in the *Supplement* to which the content of the question refers. Create a 40-question examination by choosing 10 questions from each group. You must use all of the questions in Group 4.

An Answer Key is on the page after the 60 questions, followed by Instructions for Taking the Lifeguard Training Test and an Answer Sheet. Make copies of the Instructions and the Answer Sheet for each participant and hand them out in Session 9 with each written examination.

Instructions for Taking the Lifeguard Training Test

IMPORTANT: Read all instructions before beginning this test.

INSTRUCTIONS: Mark all answers in pencil on the separate answer sheet. **Do not write on this test.** The questions on this test are multiple choice. Read each question slowly and carefully. Then choose the **best** answer and fill in that circle on the answer sheet. If you wish to change an answer, erase your first answer completely. Return this test to your instructor when you are finished.

EXAMPLE

ANSWER SHEET

16.   ●

---

16. A trained lifeguard must—
    a. Be able to recognize and deal with dangerous or potentially dangerous situations.
    b. Know how to carry out emergency plans.
    c. Continually train in order to be physically fit and mentally alert.
    d. All of the above.

Lifeguard Training Instructor Manual
Bank of Test Questions

Group 1

1. (2) The most important responsibility of a lifeguard is —
   a. To test the pH of pool water.
   b. To know and enforce facility rules.
   c. To ensure that rescue equipment is in good condition.
   d. To ensure the safety of facility patrons.

2. (3) To get a job as a lifeguard, a person typically needs—
   a. Swimming, writing, and first aid skills.
   b. Swimming, first aid, and CPR skills.
   c. Swimming, sprinting, and verbal skills.
   d. First aid, CPR, and verbal skills.

3. (3) In-service training for lifeguards includes—
   a. Becoming aware of hazardous areas at a facility.
   b. Physical conditioning and training.
   c. Learning about the legal aspects of the job.
   d. All of the above.

4. (4) To practice preventive lifeguarding effectively, lifeguards must—
   a. Be thoroughly familiar with search and recovery procedures and equipment.
   b. Be able to fill out an accident/injury or incident report.
   c. Be aware at all times of what is going on in their area of authority.
   d. Memorize the "chain of command" of the facility where they work.

5. (4) The most important factor to consider when relieving a lifeguard is—
   a. Giving him or her instructions as to duties while on break.
   b. Making sure he or she leaves all necessary equipment.
   c. Maintaining supervision of areas of responsibility.
   d. Making sure he or she is relieved on time as determined by the schedule.

6. (4) Back-up coverage is —
   a. Not important as long as a trained lifeguard is present at all times.
   b. Only important for beaches.
   c. Provided when there are two or more lifeguards on duty—one lifeguard to rescue, others to give assistance.
   d. Provided when one lifeguard is on call at home and one lifeguard is on duty.

7. (4) The placement and positioning of lifeguards and lifeguard stands are—
   a. Important to proper supervision of an aquatic facility.
   b. Influenced by the size and shape of the facility, the number of lifeguards, and the number of patrons.
   c. Adjusted based on environmental conditions.
   d. All of the above.

8. (4) How should lifeguards deal with hazardous areas at their facility?
   a. Lifeguards should whistle every time anyone goes near a hazardous area.
   b. Lifeguards should not be concerned about hazardous areas because they are trained for emergencies.
   c. Lifeguards should identify, supervise, and attempt to correct hazardous areas.
   d. Lifeguards should keep hazardous areas secret so patrons won't be alarmed.

9. (4) When enforcing rules, a lifeguard should—
   a. Briefly explain the reasons for the rules.
   b. Be fair, consistent, and equal.
   c. Take the age of a person who breaks a rule into consideration when deciding the method of enforcement.
   d. All of the above.

10. (4) The disadvantage of zone coverage by lifeguards is that—
    a. Lifeguards may be confused as to their area of responsibility.
    b. Lifeguards can only concentrate on a limited area.
    c. Lifeguards overlap coverage of the pool.
    d. Special chairs are needed.

11. (4) A disadvantage of an elevated lifeguard stand is—
    a. The chance of injury when the lifeguard has to get down in a hurry.
    b. It provides a poorer field of vision.
    c. More direct sun rays strike it.
    d. The lifeguard is too far away from the water.

12. (5) An emergency action plan for a one-lifeguard facility—
    a. Depends on an effective communications system and education of patrons.
    b. Provides a method for calling in extra lifeguards.
    c. Is not allowed by law.
    d. Should not involve police, fire, and emergency medical services personnel.

13. (5) Which signal indicates "help needed"?
    a. A rescue tube held vertically overhead and moved from side to side
    b. Arm straight out with palm facing individual
    c. A yellow flag
    d. A hand placed on top of head

14. (6)   Information given in an accident report should **not** include—

a.   Personal opinions or assumptions.
b.   Rescue, assistance, or aid given.
c.   Narrative statements by witnesses.
d.   Conditions at the time of the accident

15. (5)   Points to consider when developing a facility emergency action plan are—

a.   State and local ordinances.
b.   Posting EMS and other emergency numbers.
c.   Crowd control.
d.   All of the above.

16. (5)   A swimmer in distress at a multistaff facility needs immediate assistance. The first lifeguard goes into the water. What is the immediate responsibility of the second lifeguard?

a.   Enter the water to help the first lifeguard
b.   Supervise the area of the facility that is unattended
c.   Go call EMS immediately
d.   Get rescue equipment

17. (4)   Which formula can be used to establish lifeguard-to-patron ratios?

a.   X number of lifeguards per x number of patrons in the facility.
b.   X number of patrons on the total deck area.
c.   X number of patrons per x square feet of the surface area of the total facility.
d.   X number of patrons within x feet of the diving board.

18. (5) For communication, flags of different colors are especially useful to—
    a. Show when assistance is needed.
    b. Tell about swimming and boating conditions at a waterfront.
    c. Replace hand signals at pools.
    d. Indicate water depth at pools.

Group 2

1. (7) A backboard—
    a. Is almost never used in in-service training programs.
    b. Does not need to be made from quality material.
    c. Is not necessary equipment at an aquatic facility.
    d. Must be standard rescue equipment at all aquatic facilities.

2. (7) What is the single most important aspect of balanced water?
    a. The level of chlorine
    b. The pH factor
    c. The number of patrons
    d. The filtration system

3. (8) What should patrons be required to do to protect the healthfulness and sanitation of an aquatic facility?
    a. Eat in a separate area
    b. Stay out of the pool when the filtration system is being monitored
    c. Shower before entering the pool
    d. Pick up litter around the pool

4. (8) Which of the following is true of the water at a pool facility?
    a. It needs to have pH put in regularly.
    b. It needs to be checked for aquatic life and animal management.
    c. It needs to be chemically tested every day.
    d. It needs sun and high temperatures to remain algae-free.

5. (9) In making a water rescue, the lifeguard should use rescue equipment whenever possible because—
    a. It helps the lifeguard get into direct contact with the victim.
    b. It provides flotation for the victim or the rescuer.
    c. It allows the lifeguard less freedom of movement while towing the victim.
    d. It always allows the victim to be totally out of the water.

6. (9) Why is a rescue board better than a surfboard for rescue purposes?
    a. It can be paddled more rapidly.
    b. It is smaller.
    c. It can support two people.
    d. It is made of fiberglass.

7. (9) You have located a scuba diver in distress. What is the first step in rescuing him or her?
    a. Release the weight belt.
    b. Inflate the BCD (buoyancy compensation device).
    c. Hold the diver's head in-line with the body.
    d. Bring the diver to the surface.

8. (9) Lifeguards should not attempt swimming rescues in cold water—
    a. Without assistance and rescue equipment.
    b. Without a wet suit.
    c. Without thermoclines present.
    d. Without rescue boats and a team of scuba divers.

9. (9) When lifting a victim from the water, a lifeguard should—
   a. Always maintain contact with the victim.
   b. Use the legs as a source of power, not the back.
   c. Protect the victim's head and take care not to twist the back.
   d. All of the above.

10. (9) One difference between a passive and an active drowning victim is that—
   a. An active victim is quiet but a passive victim shouts for help.
   b. An active victim floats on his or her back, but a passive victim treads water.
   c. An active victim struggles, but a passive victim slips under water with little or no warning.
   d. An active victim slips under water with little or no warning, but a passive victim struggles.

11. (10) Which of the following are important considerations in organizing a search and rescue?
   a. Crowd control and supervision of bathers and maintenance personnel.
   b. Recruitment and training of volunteers.
   c. Establishing communication systems
   d. All of the above

12. (10) A graphic description of the shoreline and the land under water is called—
   a. A topographic map.
   b. A contour and terrain map.
   c. An area map
   d. A geological map.

13. (11) If you see lightning and count 35 seconds between its sighting and the thunder, the distance to the storm is approximately—
   a. 8 miles.
   b. 7 miles.
   c. 5 miles.
   d. 4 miles

14. (11) What should facility patrons and lifeguards do during a thunderstorm?
   a. Get inside a large building.
   b. Find shelter underneath a large tree.
   c. Ignore it because lightning is rarely produced by such storms.
   d. Have patrons find shelter in structures that are in open areas, such as picnic shelters.

15. (12) At a waterfront area—
   a. Scuba diving and boating should be allowed in the same area.
   b. The first aid station must be placed far away from the swimming area.
   c. Swimmers of different levels of swimming ability should swim in separate areas.
   d. The bottom should drop off sharply from shallow water to deep water.

Group 3

1. (S.1) When using a crawl stroke to approach a victim, you
    should—
    a. Swim more slowly as you get closer to the victim.
    b. Keep your head out of the water so you can constantly
        watch the victim.
    c. Lift your head occasionally while breathing and refocus
        on the victim.
    d. Never lift your head out of the water, in order to
        maximize speed.

2. (S.1) Which is the best approach to use when rescuing an
    active victim?
    a. A front-underwater approach.
    b. A tired-swimmer's approach on the surface.
    c. A rear approach on the surface or underwater.
    d. A front surface approach.

3. (S.1) What surface dive is safest to use when you don't know
    the water depth?
    a. The pike surface dive
    b. The quick surface dive
    c. The feetfirst surface dive
    d. The stride jump

4. (S.1) When making a throwing assist, always—
    a. Throw the device with your right hand.
    b. Lean towards the victim while you pull him or her to
        safety.
    c. Throw the line or device just beyond the victim but
        within reach.
    d. Hold the device and all of the line in the same hand.

5. (S.1) Which is **not** one of the kicks primarily used when
     rescuing a victim?
   a.   Rotary kick
   b.   Dolphin kick
   c.   Inverted scissors kick
   d.   Elementary backstroke kick

6. (S.2) When wearing snorkeling equipment, how would you
     enter water more than 8 feet deep?
   a.   · Sit-in entry
   b.   Beach entry
   c.   Feetfirst surface dive
   d.   Shallow dive

7. (S.2) To relieve ear pressure when wearing a mask—
   a.   Tilt the mask away from your face.
   b.   Press the mask against your nose and attempt to exhale.
   c.   Inhale through your nose.
   d.   Press the top of the face plate against your forehead.

8. (S.2) Which is the most common kick to use with fins?
   a.   The inverted scissors kick.
   b.   The backstroke kick.
   c.   The rotary kick.
   d.   The modified flutter kick.

9. (S.3) If you see a victim go under as you are approaching—
   a.   Surface dive at the spot where you last saw the victim on
         the surface.
   b.   Go back to shore and call EMS.
   c.   Rely on the observations of eyewitnesses to help you
         find the victim.
   d.   Wait for a team of scuba divers to come help you.

10. (S.3) When should a front-surface approach be used with a victim?

    a.   When the victim is facedown at or near the surface

    b.   When the victim is active and panicky

    c.   When the victim has a spinal injury

    d.   When the victim is tired but can follow directions

11. (S.3) A properly performed wrist tow—

    a.   Can be used on an active or passive victim.

    b.   Is used if the victim grabs the rescuer's hand.

    c.   Can only be used with an underwater approach.

    d.   Is only used for a passive victim.

12. (S.3) The first thing you should do if you are grabbed around the head by a distressed swimmer is to—

    a.   Tuck and turn your chin.

    b.   Take a breath.

    c.   Try to shake free.

    d.   Submerge.

13. (S.3) What is the best rescue method for a single lifeguard to use with two near-drowning victims clutching each other who are close to safety?

    a.   Separate the victims immediately.

    b.   Tow one victim to safety and come back for the other one.

    c.   Push both victims underwater to separate them.

    d.   Tow or push the victims clutching each other to safety.

14. (S.3) Rescue breathing in deep water is extremely difficult without—

    a.   The modified jaw thrust.

    b.   Flotation equipment.

    c.   Available resuscitation equipment.

    d.   An emergency action plan.

15. (S.3) Where do you grasp the victim when performing a front head-hold or rear head-hold escape?
    a. By the head and shoulders
    b. By the wrists
    c. By the elbows or upper arms
    d. By the shoulders or neck

16. (S.3) If a victim grasps you firmly by the upper arm, you should—
    a. Submerge and try to swim away.
    b. Allow the victim to hang on until you get tired.
    c. Use the backstroke to swim to safety.
    d. Block the victim and use your free hand to submerge the victim.

17. (S.3) If a distressed swimmer suddenly tries to grab you, your first reaction should be to use the—
    a. Front head-hold escape.
    b. Rear head-hold escape.
    c. One-hand or two-hand block.
    d. Wrist/arm escape.

Group 4

1. (S.4) The technique of stabilizing a victim's spine is known as—
    a. Neck stabilization.
    b. Arm/head stabilization.
    c. In-line stabilization.
    d. Shoulder/head stabilization.

2. (S.4) Approximately 95 per cent of diving injuries occur in water that is—
    a. Over 10 feet deep.
    b. Less than 10 feet deep.
    c. Over 5 feet deep.
    d. Less than 5 feet deep.

3. (S.4) Signs and symptoms of possible spinal injury include—
   a. Tingling or numbness in the extremities.
   b. Unconsciousness.
   c. Distortion of the neck.
   d. All of the above.

4. (S.5) When rescuing a victim of a seizure in the water, your first step is to—
   a. Support the victim so breathing is possible.
   b. Remove the victim quickly.
   c. Throw the victim a ring buoy.
   d. Carry a rescue tube out for the victim to hang on to.

5. (S.4) The correct sequence of rescue procedures for a victim of a suspected spinal injury is—
   a. Check for breathing, stabilize the spine, and remove from the water.
   b. Activate the facility emergency plan, approach the victim carefully, and reduce any movement of the victim's spine.
   c. Approach the victim carefully, remove the victim from the water, and check for breathing.
   d. Secure the victim to a backboard, check for breathing, and keep the victim warm.

6. (S.4) When no immediate help is available, the simplest support in shallow water for a faceup victim of a suspected spinal injury is—
   a. Hip and foot support.
   b. Hip and shoulder support.
   c. Head and chin support.
   d. Head splint technique.

7. (S.4) Use of the head/chin support technique requires the rescuer to apply pressure to the victim's spine and chest with his or her—

    a. Hands.
    b. Wrists.
    c. Forearms.
    d. Shoulders.

8. (S.5) Treatment for mild to moderate hypothermia includes—

    a. Moving victim to a warm area; getting victim into dry clothing; giving warm liquids to a conscious victim.
    b. Moving victim indoors; placing victim in front of fan for increased air circulation; putting warm clothes on victim.
    c. Giving warm liquids; keeping victim in water; increasing victim's exercise.
    d. Giving warm coffee; getting victim out of water; dressing victim lightly.

9. (S.4) When assessing a victim's injuries, in which situation would you suspect a spinal injury?

    a. Any fall from a height greater than the victim's.
    b. Any victim found unconscious or submerged in shallow water for unknown reasons.
    c. Any victim with significant head trauma.
    d. All of the above.

10. (S.5) Which of the following factors influence the onset and progression of hypothermia?

    a. The individual's age, body size, and body build.
    b. The air and water temperature.
    c. The length of exposure.
    d. All of the above.

AMERICAN RED CROSS Lifeguard Training
Answer Sheet

Name _____ Test _____

DIRECTIONS: Fill in the correct answer for each question.

1.	ⓐ	ⓑ	ⓒ	ⓓ		21.	ⓐ	ⓑ	ⓒ	ⓓ
2.	ⓐ	ⓑ	ⓒ	ⓓ		22.	ⓐ	ⓑ	ⓒ	ⓓ
3.	ⓐ	ⓑ	ⓒ	ⓓ		23.	ⓐ	ⓑ	ⓒ	ⓓ
4.	ⓐ	ⓑ	ⓒ	ⓓ		24.	ⓐ	ⓑ	ⓒ	ⓓ
5.	ⓐ	ⓑ	ⓒ	ⓓ		25.	ⓐ	ⓑ	ⓒ	ⓓ
6.	ⓐ	ⓑ	ⓒ	ⓓ		26.	ⓐ	ⓑ	ⓒ	ⓓ
7.	ⓐ	ⓑ	ⓒ	ⓓ		27.	ⓐ	ⓑ	ⓒ	ⓓ
8.	ⓐ	ⓑ	ⓒ	ⓓ		28.	ⓐ	ⓑ	ⓒ	ⓓ
9.	ⓐ	ⓑ	ⓒ	ⓓ		29.	ⓐ	ⓑ	ⓒ	ⓓ
10.	ⓐ	ⓑ	ⓒ	ⓓ		30.	ⓐ	ⓑ	ⓒ	ⓓ
11.	ⓐ	ⓑ	ⓒ	ⓓ		31.	ⓐ	ⓑ	ⓒ	ⓓ
12.	ⓐ	ⓑ	ⓒ	ⓓ		32.	ⓐ	ⓑ	ⓒ	ⓓ
13.	ⓐ	ⓑ	ⓒ	ⓓ		33.	ⓐ	ⓑ	ⓒ	ⓓ
14.	ⓐ	ⓑ	ⓒ	ⓓ		34.	ⓐ	ⓑ	ⓒ	ⓓ
15.	ⓐ	ⓑ	ⓒ	ⓓ		35.	ⓐ	ⓑ	ⓒ	ⓓ
16.	ⓐ	ⓑ	ⓒ	ⓓ		36.	ⓐ	ⓑ	ⓒ	ⓓ
17.	ⓐ	ⓑ	ⓒ	ⓓ		37.	ⓐ	ⓑ	ⓒ	ⓓ
18.	ⓐ	ⓑ	ⓒ	ⓓ		38.	ⓐ	ⓑ	ⓒ	ⓓ
19.	ⓐ	ⓑ	ⓒ	ⓓ		39.	ⓐ	ⓑ	ⓒ	ⓓ
20.	ⓐ	ⓑ	ⓒ	ⓓ		40.	ⓐ	ⓑ	ⓒ	ⓓ

You may wish to go back and check your answers to be sure that you matched the right answer with the right question.

Appendix J
Final Skills Test Checklist
Session 9

Instructor: _____

Course Date(s) and Time(s): _____

This checklist can be reproduced and used each time you teach the course. Put a P in the box next to each participant's name when that participant passes the skill test.

Name of Participant	Stride/Jump Wrist Tow	Dive to Rear Armpit Tow	Rear Approach Cross-Chest Carry	Tread Water Holding Brick	1- and 2-Hand Block	Wrist-Grip Escape	Rear Head-Hold Escape	Front Head-Hold Escape
1.								
2.								
3.								
4.								
5.								
6.								
7.								
8.								
9.								
10.								
11.								
12.								
13.								
14.								
15.								

Appendix J
Final Skills Test Checklist
Session 10

Instructor: _____

Course Date(s) and Time(s): _____

This checklist can be reproduced and used each time you teach the course. Put a P in the box next to each participant's name when that participant passes the skill test.

Name of Participant	Shallow Dive (25 yd, approach) 18 sec.	Spinal, Shallow Water (turn and support victim)	Spinal, Deep Water (turn and support victim)	Shallow Dive (10 yd. approach/9 ft. surface dive, recover brick/return)11 sec.	Rescue Tube (20 yds., tow to safety, rescue breathing)	Shallow Dive (25 yd. Sprint, get brick, and return) 1 min., 10 sec.
1.						
2.						
3.						
4.						
5.						
6.						
7.						
8.						
9.						
10.						
11.						
12.						
13.						
14.						
15.						